KB196862

NEW

교원임용시험 전공영어 대비 [제1판]

Build Up

박문각 임용

동영상강의 www.pmg.co.kr

박현수 영어교육론 **I**-1

Guideline for Pre-service Teachers
Theoretical Background for Classroom Teaching

박문각

Preface

올 한 해는 한강 작가의 영예로운 노벨 문학상 소식과 평소 존경하던 Banksy의 전시도 있었던 해인지라 너무도 영광스럽게 기억될 듯합니다. 또한, 개인적으로는 오랜 인연과의 이별로 서로의 안녕을 위해 정리하는 시간이기도 해서 아쉽게 기억될 듯도 합니다. 항상 수많은 인연들 속에 묻혀서 만나고 떠나는 시간 속에 있는 저이지만 쉬운 이별은 없는 것 같습니다.

그렇게 1년 동안 죽도록 살가운 여러분을 보내고 또 새로운 여러분을 만나며 강의를 시작했던 시간 속에서 제 자신을 다시 뒤돌아보며 너무도 열정이 넘쳤던 노량진의 첫 시절을 떠올리게 되었습니다. 어느 해 겨울, 힘들어하던 수강생의 마음이 안쓰러워 새벽 3시까지 전화를 잡고 이야기를 나누며 하나가 되었던 마음들, 그렇게 인연을 쌓아가며 시간은 어느새 24년이 흘러 지금 이 자리에 있습니다.

"안녕하세요, 교수님! 작년 1, 2차 강의를 수강한 강*준 학생이라고 합니다. 2024학년도 서울 임용에 합격하여 오늘 자로 발령을 받았다는 기쁜 소식을 전해드리고 싶어서 연락드렸습니다.^^ 제가 초수라 많이 부족했지만 교수님께서 만들어주신 12번의 모의고사를 치며 크게 발전할 수 있었습니다. 2024년에는 교수님께 받은 사랑과 관심을 학생들에게 나누어줄 수 있도록 하겠습니다! 정말 감사드립니다."

"안녕하세요, 교수님! 기억하실지는 모르겠지만, 7월부터 직강 들으면서 올해 시험 준비한 김*정이라고 합니다! 연락이 정말 늦었지만, 제가 이번에 부산 지역 공립 신규 임용에 합격하게 되었습니다.! 전화로 직접 말씀드리고 싶었지만, 바쁘실 거 같아 카톡으로 대신합니다..ㅎㅎ 4월에 전화상담을 한번 한 적이 있었는데 그때 교수님께서 1년 동안의 공부 방향을 잘 잡아주셔서 초반부터 마음잡고 공부할 수 있었던 것 같습니다. 인강을 들을 때보다 직강을 들으니 교수님께서 얼마나 열정적이고 학생들에게 애정을 가지고 가르쳐주시는지 느껴져서 더 열심히 공부할 수 있었습니다.! 정말 정말 감사합니다.!"

숨가쁘게 9~11월을 보내고 수업실연에 넋을 잃고 있을 즈음 반갑게 받게 되는 여러분의 기쁜 소식이 또 지치는 줄 모르고 한 해를 힘차게 시작하게 만들기도 합니다.

또다시 Build-up I, II의 개정 작업을 진행하면서 그 시간이 새록새록 저의 열정을 깨우기도 했습니다. 바쁜 모의고사 시간 속에서도 2025년에 만날 여러분을 생각하니 조력자로서 도움이 되어야겠다는 생각에 Build-up I은 조금 더 폭 넓게 교육론의 전반적인 이해를 이끌어 나가기 위해 지엽적인 자료를 과감하게 삭제하고, 보다 핵심적인 강의를 할 수 있도록 정리했습니다. 반면에 Build-up II는 전면적인 개정을 진행했습니다. 매년 모의고사때 답안 쓰는 것에 어려움을 느끼는 예비 선생님들을 볼 때마다 조금 더 일찍 data-processing이나 direction analysis를 접하는 것이 필요하다는 생각을 떨칠 수 없어서 이번에는 마음먹고 4월 강의부터 진행해 봐야겠다는 심산으로 과감하게 Build-up II를 Worksheet의 형태로 구성했습니다.

2025년 New Build-up I, II는 2025년 대비 중등 임용 기출을 토대로 2022년 개정 교육과정과 2025년 중고등 과정의 새로운 변화인 AIDT(AI DIGITAL TEXTBOOK), 최소 성취 기준 달성에 초점을 둔 교실 수업 방식, 마지막으로 교실 안에서 교수와 학습의 형태를 시각화시킬 수 있도록 강의 맞춤으로 구성했습니다.

2025년 New Build-up I, II에 대한 정리와 개정을 위해 애써주신 영어교육론 드림팀 선임연구원 박옥진과 유다현 선생님께 무한한 감사를 드리며, 늘 강의에 몰입할 수 있도록 건강한 팀워크를 만들어주신 유희태 선생님과 바쁘신 와중에도 통합 문제 자료를 일목요연하게 정리해주신 앤드류 선생님께 무한한 감사를 드립니다. 무엇보다 이번 Build-up I, II가 나올 수 있도록 아낌없는 노력과 소통을 해주신 변수경 편집위원에게도 특별한 감사를 전합니다.

또한, 2024년 12월까지 너무도 애를 많이 써준 연주, 소진, 정인, 주영, 혜원 그리고 영석이에게 너희들이 있어서 연구실이 밝고 긍정적인 에너지가 넘쳤고 연구실에 오는 것이 소풍처럼 늘 즐거웠다는 걸 말해주고 싶어^^

끝으로 2024년에도 바쁜 와이프 대신 간장게장과 새우장을 담가주고 심지어 무생채까지 만들어 맛있게 먹게 해준 너그러운 나의 신랑 박상준, 기후변화 전문가의 바쁜 스케줄에도 시간을 쪼개 가족을 위해 헌신하는 당신의 사랑과 이제 스무 살을 훌쩍 넘어가며 자신의 길에 대한 고민을 하고 2025년 한 해를 더 기대하게 만드는 우리 딸, 세현 양의 효도를 받으며 그렇게 기쁘고 건강한 2025년이 채워지리라 기대해봅니다.

2024년 12월에

박희수

Guide

2025학년도 기출분석 및 2026학년도 대비 영어교육론 시험 전략

2025학년도 중등 임용시험의 영어교육론은 총 23문항 중 2024학년 기출 문항수(11문항)보다 한 문항 적은 10문항이 출제되어 총 80점 중 36점을 차지하였다. 여전히 교사 시험답게 영어교육론의 출제 비중이 50%에 달하는 것을 확인할 수 있다. 이것은 중등 임용시험의 정체성에 따라 영어교사의 필수 자질인 how to teach에 대한 자필평가의 중요성을 반영한 것으로 판단된다. 2025학년도 중등 임용시험은 전년도에 비해 비교적 난이도가 중/중하로 구성된 문항들이 출제되었으며, data-based item과 knowledge-based item이 기입형과 서술형에 고르게 출제되었다. 우선, 2025학년도 중등 임용 출제 방향을 살펴보면 첫째, 2022년 개정 교육과정의 주요 학습 개념인 Project-based learning과 digital literacy가 반영된 것을 확인할 수 있다. 둘째, 학생 중심 교실 수업을 계획할 수 있는 교사의 자질에 대한 평가로써 material adaptation, lesson objectives 및 modified lesson의 방식과 특징들이 출제되었다. 셋째, 학생 측면에서는 중간언어 형태의 특징과 reading strategies 등의 유무에 초점을 두어 출제되었으며, 마지막으로 언어학습의 최종 목표가 목표 문화의 수용이라는 측면에서 매년 문화지도가 출제되는 경향이 있는데 이번에도 역시 문화지도에 대한 내용이 출제되었다.

A형 기입형 문항

기입형 3, 4번은 예년보다는 평이한 개념이자 반복적으로 출제된 term인 'modifying'과 'inter-rater reliability'를 묻는 문항이 출제되었다. 이때 3번의 경우, term 도출 방식은 Original Material을 토대로 Adapted Material에 어떤 변화가 있는지 살펴보고, 해당 변화를 설명한 term을 data에서 고르는 방식으로 출제되었다. 4번의 term인 'inter-rater reliability'는 두 선생님의 대화 내용과 Mr. Lee의 Teaching Journal로 유추하여 찾을 수 있으며, comments에 나온 definition으로 해당 term을 확정할 수 있다. 다만, 4번은 data에서 찾아 쓰는 data-matching 방식으로 term을 도출했던 3번과 달리 example이나 situation, definition을 보고 해당 개념을 정확히 도출하는 knowledge-based 방식의 문항이다.

A형 서술형 문항

- 8번(data-based item)은 〈A〉에 학생들의 중간언어 발전 단계에 대한 L2 학생들의 다양한 변이적인 중간언어 형태에 관련된 설명과 예시를 data로 주고, 〈B〉에서 제공한 학생 대화와 matching하는 문항이다.
- 9번(data-based item)은 말하기 평가 원리에 관한 문항으로, 〈A〉에서 4개의 평가 원리를 제시하고 〈B〉에서 Mr. Jeong이 Item 1과 2에서 평가한 사례를 보고 matching하는 문항이다.
- 11번(knowledge-based item)은 〈A〉에서 각각 듣기/읽기와 말하기/쓰기에 대한 수업 목표를 제시하고, 〈B〉의 Teaching Procedure에서 제시되는 활동과의 관계를 파악하는 문항이다.
- 12번(data-based item)은 〈A〉에서 다양한 Reading Strategies에 대한 category를 제시하고 〈B〉에서 학생들의 읽기에 대한 문제점을 제공하여, 이를 해결할 수 있는 Reading Strategies를 고르는 문항이다.

B형 서술형 문항

- 6번(data-based item)은 〈A〉에 2022년 개정 교육과정의 핵심 교수 방법 중 하나인 Project-based learning에 대한 학습 단계가 제시되었고, 〈B〉에 실제 일정 기간(1st Week~6th Week)의 교실 수업 단계가 제시되어 두 단계 간의 mismatching을 묻는 문항이다.
- 7번(knowledge-based item)은 〈A〉에 제시된 초임교사와 주임교사 간 대화로 효율적인 수업을 위한 수업 계획 수정(modified lesson)에 관련된 문항으로, intensive listening을 이해하고 creative writing에 대한 개념을 묻는 문항이다.

- 10번(data-based item)은 다년간 중등 임용시험에서 주요 토픽으로 다루고 있는 문화학습 관련 문항이다. ⟨A⟩에서 문화학습 과정인 noticing, comparing, reflecting, interacting의 개념들과 두 학생의 문화학습 단계를 보여주는 발화 간 matching을 묻고 있고, ⟨B⟩에서는 두 학생의 대화로 알 수 있는 문화학습 과정을 규명하는 문항이다.
- 11번 문항(knowledge-based item)은 ⟨A⟩에 how to use digital tools에 대한 원리를 제시하고, ⟨B⟩에서 8차 시간 수업 중 원리 mismatching에 대한 것을 고르는 문항이다. 이 문항은 discovery learning과 drill 간의 차이와 individualized feedback의 이해 여부를 묻는 문항이다.

2025학년도 대비 중등 임용 영어교육론의 방향

A형과 B형의 문항 유형에서 살펴봤듯이, 2025년 기출의 가장 큰 특징은 실제 교실 수업에서 교사의 자질과 학생들의 주도적 학습을 위한 교실 계획 및 언어학습의 궁극적인 목적인 목표 문화학습으로 꼽을 수 있다. 중등 임용시험에서 영어교육론의 난이도는 문학과 영어학 등 다른 영역에 비하면 중간 정도의 익숙한 문항들이 출제되고 있으나, 다른 내용학의 어려움에 대한 득점 손실을 만회할 수 있도록 영어교육론의 감점을 최소화하는 전략을 2026년 대비 중등 임용의 핵심 전략으로 삼아야 할 것이다. 이 목표를 성취하기 위해서는 영어교육론의 개념을 폭넓게 이해하고, 실전 문항의 data-processing / direction analysis/ correct answer에 대한 연습을 상반기부터 진행해야 한다.

2025학년도 기출 **전공A 기입형**

03. Read the passage and follow the directions. [2 points]

Materials can be adapted by using different techniques such as *adding, deleting, modifying,* and *reordering.* For example, we can add materials when a language item is not covered sufficiently in the original materials. Materials that are too easy or difficult for learners can be deleted. Modifying can be used to make them more relevant to students' interests and backgrounds and to restructure classroom management. Reordering the sequence of activities is another technique, which includes separating items and regrouping them.

Consider the original material extracted from a grammar exercise book and its adapted version below. In the adapted version, the original exercise has been adapted by using the ① _____ technique.

Original Material

❶ **[Individual Work]** Describe the man's routine in four sentences.

_____

_____

Guide

❷ **[Individual Work]** Answer the following questions.

What time do you wake up?

What do you usually wear to work?

What do you usually cook for dinner?

Adapted Material

❶ **[Individual Work]** Describe the student's routine in four sentences.

❷ **[Pair Work]** Work in pairs and ask each other the following questions.

What time do you wake up?

What do you usually wear on school days?

What do you usually eat for dinner?

Fill in the blank ① with the ONE most appropriate word from the passage.

모범답안 modifying

2025학년도 기출 ｜ 전공A 기입형

04. Read the conversation in <A> and the passage in <B>, and follow the directions. [2 points]

─────┤ **A** ├─────

(Two teachers, Mr. Lee and Ms. Kim, recently scored students' speaking assessments. They later discussed the scoring process and Mr. Lee reflected on his scoring experiences in his journals.)

Mr. Lee : As I was reviewing my ratings, I noticed that they were staying consistent throughout the scoring process.

Ms. Kim : Good, it's actually hard to keep the same perspective when grading multiple students. But you mean you found actual similarities in your scores for the same students over time?

Mr. Lee : Yes, exactly. I think I might have benefitted from reviewing my previous scores before re-evaluating anyone's performance to see if I'm staying consistent.

Ms. Kim : That makes sense. You know, I've noticed that we have some scoring differences between us on certain criteria.

Mr. Lee : Right. I normally give a score of 10 if students have natural flow even though they may demonstrate some errors in grammar or vocabulary. How about you?

Ms. Kim : Oh, I've constantly made efforts to adhere to our scoring criteria, and I give a perfect score only when they speak without any errors or hesitation.

Mr. Lee : All right. Now I can see why we have different scoring results and it makes me think—these different results could send mixed messages to students.

Ms. Kim : I agree. Let's review our criteria and stick to following our rubric.

Mr. Lee : Sure. That would be fairer for the students.

B

Mr. Lee's Reflective Journal

After today's grading session, I reviewed my scores and luckily noticed consistency in my ratings for the same students across different sessions. However, after talking with Ms. Kim, I realized that we provided different scores for the same students. I'm concerned this could lead to some confusion if they receive different scores based on which teacher assesses them. I think it would be helpful if Ms. Kim and I could go over the rubric together to ensure a more unified scoring approach.

Fill in the blanks with the TWO most appropriate words.

Based on <A> and <B>, Mr. Lee is concerned about the lack of _____ _____ in the scoring process. His concern is not about the consistency of rating by a single rater but about the consistency of rating by different raters.

모범답안 inter-rater reliability

08. Read the passage in <A> and the conversation in <B>, and follow the directions. [4 points]

A

Understanding second language (L2) learners' interlanguage is an important step for teaching L2 learners. In analyzing interlanguage, it has been found that deviations from characteristics of the target language exist in learners' utterances. For example, deviations in early L2 learners' utterances can be categorized into several types.

<Deviations in Early L2 Learners' Utterances>

Type	Description	Example (The intended meaning is in parentheses.)
Mismatched lexical class	The lexical class does not match.	*It's a pink.* (It's pink.)
Semantic deviation	Utterances are semantically ill-formed.	*What's the spaghetti?* (Do you like spaghetti?)
Number of arguments	Utterances contain more or fewer arguments than required.	*I wore.* (I wore a shirt.)
Word order	Word order is violated.	*I this book read.* (I read this book.)
...	...	...

B

(Two students are carrying out a two-way spot-the-difference task in their English class.)

S1: Now, let's get started. In your picture, are there chairs?
S2: Yes.
S1: How many chairs are there?
S2: Two chairs.
S1: There are also two chairs in my picture. Now, please ask me about my picture.
S2: What's the pen?
S1: I'm sorry? Do you mean, "Do you have a pen?"
S2: Yes.
S1: Okay. Then, yes, I do. Do you have a pen?
S2: No, I do not have a pen.
S1: Okay. Then we've found one difference. Next, your turn.
S2: Is there a girl?
S1: Yes, there is. What is she doing?
S2: She is giving Mary.
S1: Um, what is she giving Mary?
S2: Ah, she is giving Mary a book.
S1: Oh, in my picture, she is giving Mary an eraser.
S2: Yeah! Finally, we got them all.

Note: S=student

Based on <A>, identify the TWO types of deviations found in the students' utterances in <B>. Then, explain your answers, respectively, with evidence from <B>.

(모범답안) In the conversation, S2 demonstrates 'Semantic deviation' and a deviation in the 'Number of arguments'. First, S2 produces the ill-formed utterance. 'What's the pen?' instead of the intended meaning. "Do you have a pen?". Additionally, S2 says "She is giving Mary," Where the necessary arguments. 'a book' is omitted.

2025학년도 기출 | 전공A 서술형

09. Read the passage in <A> and the teacher's reflection log in <B>, and follow the directions. [4 points]

A

Mr. Jeong, an English teacher, was tasked with evaluating speaking assessment items in his students' final exam. Reviewing key principles of speaking assessment, he noted the following:

✔ Clarity: Prompts should be straightforward to avoid confusion.
✔ Authenticity: Speaking tasks should mirror real-life communication, enabling students to demonstrate natural language use.
✔ Integrated Skills Assessment: Tasks should assess speaking alongside other skills, such as listening comprehension, to reflect communicative performance.
✔ Practicality: Test items should be feasible and manageable in terms of the time spent in assessment.

B

Teacher's Reflection Log

After reviewing the items, I felt that the two items had some good and bad points. Item 1 asked students to describe a memorable experience that they had with a friend, including details such as when it happened, what they did, and why it was memorable. After observing students' responses, I realized that this item resembled a conversation topic in real-life contexts. However, I regret that I didn't set time limits for the item and it took too much time to score it, which made the assessment difficult to manage.

For Item 2, after looking at a picture of a busy street, students were asked to describe what they saw. Most of the students did very well on this task because the item clearly described what sort of response was desired. I think this item was effective in assessing pronunciation, one of the criteria for assessing speaking skills. However, next time I want to add some more items such as asking students to listen to a short audio and discuss their opinions. It might be more challenging but I believe I can assess multiple skills in the test.

Based on <A>, identify the speaking assessment principles applied in Item 1 and Item 2 in <B>, respectively. Then, explain how each principle was applied in each item with evidence from <B>.

(모범답안) Authenticity is applied to Item 1 because the conversation topic about memorable experience with friends reflects real-life contexts. On the other hand, Clarity is applied to Item 2, because the use of a prompt. 'a picture of a busy street', enables students to clearly describe what they observed.

11. Read the passage in <A> and the teaching procedure in <B>, and follow the directions. [4 points]

A

Ms. Kim, an English teacher, is selecting lesson objectives to implement into a new lesson. The following are the lesson objectives for reception and production.

Lesson Objectives

Reception

R1. Students can recognize reduced sounds of words.

R2. Students can identify specific details from a text or discourse.

R3. Students can distinguish between literal and implied meanings.

Production

P1. Students can explain the sequence of an event in the right order.

P2. Students can write a simple journal, letter, or email.

P3. Students can argue for and against a topic in a respectful manner.

B

Step	Teaching Procedure
Step 1	In groups, students brainstorm the pros and cons of using AI in education and create a mind map. convenient — distracting — immediate feedback — Pros — AI — Cons — cheating — no constraints — less human interaction — place — time
Step 2	Students listen to an audio clip on AI and digital tools in class and complete a worksheet. ▶ Listen to the conversation carefully and follow the directions below. A. Mark the sentences True or False. 1. Sora says that the use of AI should be prohibited in the classroom. [True/False] 2. Inho asks an AI chatbot to do his assignment. [True/False] 3. Minji compares the outputs on a topic from three different AI chatbots. [True/False] B. Match the person with his or her concern. Inho · · Excessive screen time Minji · · False information Sora · · Theft of personal data

Step 3	Students work together and write rules for the use of digital tools in class.
	
	Class Rules for the Use of Digital Tools
	1. *e.g., Never download software to a school device without permission.*
	2. _____
	3. _____
	
	◆Useful expressions for polite agreement or disagreement
	  - I agree. That's a good idea. That's right.
	  - I don't think/believe so. I don't agree/disagree (with you).
	  - What do you think? Would you agree with me? Don't you agree?

Identify ONE lesson objective for reception and ONE lesson objective for production from <A> that the teaching procedure in <B> targets. Then, explain your answers, respectively, with evidence from <B>.

[모범답안] One objective for reception is for students to identify specific details from an audio clip by marking statements as True or False and matching a person with their specific concern. Additionally, one objective for production is for students to argue for and against a topic in a respectful manner while discussing class rules for the use of digital tools, using useful expressions for polite agreement or disagreement.

2025학년도 기출 　전공A 서술형

12. Read the passages in <A> and <B>, and follow the directions. [4 points]

---| A |---

Metacognitive awareness of reading strategies is considered a conscious procedure utilized by readers to enhance text comprehension and encourage active reading.

Understanding its importance, Ms. Yu, a high school English teacher, used the Metacognitive Awareness of Reading Strategy Questionnaire to measure students' awareness on three categories of reading strategies. These include Global Reading Strategies (GLOB), Support Reading Strategies (SUP), and Problem-Solving Strategies (PROB). She also interviewed her students after the survey.

The Metacognitive Awareness of Reading Strategy Questionnaire

Category	Item	1	2	3	4	5
GLOB	G1. I have a purpose in mind when I read.					
	G2. I think about what I know to help me understand what I read.					
	G3. While reading, I decide what to read and what to ignore.					
	G4. I take an overall view of the text to see what it is about before reading it.					
	...			...		
SUP	S1. I paraphrase what I read to better understand it.					
	S2. I take notes while reading to help me understand what I read.					
	S3. While reading, I translate from English into my native language.					
	S4. I use reference materials (e.g., a dictionary) to help me understand what I read.					
					...	
PROB	P1. When the text is unclear, I re-read it to increase my understanding.					
	P2. I try to guess the meaning of unknown words or phrases.					
	P3. I adjust my reading speed according to what I am reading.					
	P4. I try to visualize information to help understand what I read.					
	...				...	

Note: 1=never, 2=occasionally, 3=sometimes, 4=usually, 5=always

---
B

Based on the survey results, Ms. Yu conducted interviews with the students who reported low ratings in the survey. Parts of the interview excerpts are below. One of the interview questions was "Do you feel challenged while reading?" After the interview, Ms. Yu identified reading strategies that students need to promote their active reading skills.

Interview Excerpts

S1 : "I thought reading was just about understanding the words. When I don't understand something, I tend to skip over it. I think if I try to draw a picture in my mind when I'm not sure, I'll understand texts much better."

S2 : "I usually analyze texts sentence-by-sentence until I fully understand them. After checking my low ratings on the questionnaire, I found that reading selectively may help me become a more efficient reader."

Note: S=student

Identify the TWO items of reading strategies in <A> that Ms. Yu may apply to her reading instruction in relation to <B>. Then, explain your answers, respectively, with evidence from <B>.

모범답안 Ms. Yu may instruct S2s to "decide what to read and what to ignore" from G3, encouraging them to avoid analyzing texts sentence-by-sentence and instead focus on reading selectively. Additionally, she can guide S1s to "visualize information" from P4, helping them picture what they read to enhance comprehension.

2025학년도 기출 　전공B 서술형

06. Read the passages in <A> and <B>, and follow the directions. [4 points]

---| A |---

Project-based learning (PBL) is a teaching method that facilitates students to use an inquiry process with an integrated goal and interrelated subsidiary tasks. One possible procedure for implementing PBL is provided below.

Students collaboratively set the goal and scope of the project. This makes students feel in control of their own projects from the beginning. Once the goal is set, students as a group actively discuss and decide upon what to include in their project. When collecting information for the project, students develop integrated language skills in meaningful ways. Students then create their projects collaboratively with their group members. Finally, students present their projects in class. When assessing student projects, the teacher evaluates students' learning progress, focusing on the process as well as the product.

---| B |---

Referring to the procedure as described in <A>, Ms. Park, a middle school English teacher, implemented PBL into her class over six weeks. Each week, one class session was allocated for the PBL project. When each session was over, Ms. Park briefly wrote a teacher's log to record events and observations. Some entries of her logs are provided below.

Week 1

I decided on a specific goal for the project and announced it to students. The goal was to make tourist brochures and distribute them to the local communities. I assigned students to groups of four. I also provided guidelines on the project.

Week 2

The groups explored possible destinations to include in their brochures. Students also searched the Internet for various brochures and analyzed the sections within. They found details including attractions, activities, and food.

Week 3

The groups conducted a survey on their classmates' recommendations for the destination their group decided upon. They did so by asking and responding to each other. Then they summarized the survey results.

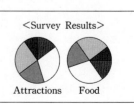

Week 4

The students worked closely in a group to make their brochures. Upon completion, they prepared for a group presentation.

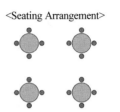
<Seating Arrangement>

Week 5

Each group gave a ten-minute presentation. Students also prepared for distributing the brochures to the local communities.

Tourist Brochure

Week 6

As the final step, I evaluated students' brochures based on a rubric, which consisted of vocabulary, grammar, and layout.

<Rubric>

Group # : _____

	1	2	3	4	5
Vocabulary					
Grammar					
Layout					

Identify the TWO weeks in <B> that do NOT follow the procedure provided in <A>. Then, explain how the identified weeks deviate from the procedure in <A>.

모범답안   Week 1 and Week 6 do not align with the PBL procedure. In Week 1, Ms. Park directly sets and announces the project goal to the students, instead of allowing them to collaboratively determine the goal and scope of the project. In Week 6, she evaluates students' learning progress based solely on the final products—brochures—without assessing both the learning process and the product.

2025학년도 기출 | 전공B 서술형

07. Read the conversation in <A> and the lesson plans in <B>, and follow the directions. [4 points]

A

(Mr. Choi, a supervising teacher, is talking with his student teacher, Ms. Han, about her lesson plan.)

SupT: Ms. Han, I checked your lesson plan and found a couple of things that may help improve it.

ST : Oh, did I miss anything?

SupT: As you know, before you get to the main listening stage, we want students to recognize the purpose of listening, right?

ST : Yeah, and it sounds quite challenging. How can I do that?

SupT: You can try activating schemata. Making connections between personal experiences and learning can facilitate students' comprehension.

ST : Oh, I see.

SupT: And I recommend intensive listening. You know, authentic conversations have a lot of contractions. So, how about playing parts of a radio show focusing on particular language features?

ST : Good idea. Thank you. Is there anything else I missed?

SupT: Hmm, why don't you also try making some creative activities? Students can sing a song or chant, or they can record their own voice.

ST : Got it. I'll try to find some that are exciting.

SupT: Great. That's all I wanted to point out.

ST : Your suggestions are extremely helpful. I'll make some changes following your advice.

SupT: If you have any questions, don't hesitate to ask.

ST : I really appreciate your advice.

Note: SupT=supervising teacher, ST=student teacher

B

After the conversation, Ms. Han revised her lesson plan based on Mr. Choi's suggestions. Below are the original and modified lesson plans.

Original Lesson Plan

Stage	Teaching & Learning Activities
Pre–listening	• T shows the aim of the listening activity. • T asks about what will happen to a person in a picture. • T engages Ss in small talk.
While–listening	• T asks Ss to listen to a story. • T asks Ss to make inferences about the main topic of the story. • T asks Ss to retell the story.
Post–listening	• T asks Ss to write a summary on the story. • T asks Ss to present on their summaries. • T provides comments on Ss' presentations.

Modified Lesson Plan

Stage	Teaching & Learning Activities
Pre–listening	• T presents the purpose of the listening activity. • T asks Ss to predict what will happen to a person in a picture. • T engages Ss in small talk.
While–listening	• T asks Ss to listen to a story. • T asks Ss to guess what the main topic of the story is. • T asks Ss to do a gap-filling activity.
Post–listening	• T asks Ss to summarize the story. • T asks Ss to act out assigned scenes from the story. • T provides feedback on Ss' performances.

Note: T=teacher, Ss=students

Identify the supervising teacher's TWO suggestions from <A> that are reflected in the modified lesson plan in <B>. Then, explain your answers, respectively, with evidence from <B>.

모범답안 The supervising teacher provides two suggestions: intensive listening and creative activities. The student teacher incorporates these suggestions into the modified lesson plan. First, during the listening activity, the original story-retelling task is replaced with a gap-filling activity. Additionally, after listening, the student teacher plans for students to act out assigned scenes instead of merely presenting their summaries.

2025학년도 기출 전공B 서술형

10. Read the passages in <A> and <B>, and follow the directions. [4 points]

A

Intercultural language learning in the classroom can be conceptualized as a series of four interrelated processes: *noticing, comparing, reflecting,* and *interacting.* First, noticing is for learners to experience new input about culture and attempt to understand it. Teachers may use various exemplifications of the target culture as input, such as videos, written texts, and cartoons. Second, comparing occurs when learners are engaged in identifying similarities and differences between learners' culture and the target culture. Third, reflecting implies that learners make personal interpretations of experiences and react to linguistic and cultural diversity. Finally, interacting involves learners communicating personal meanings about their experiences, exploring those meanings, and reshaping them in response to others.

The two excerpts below are parts of students' speeches in class.

Excerpt from Seoyeon's Speech

"I imagined what I would and wouldn't like about attending a U.S. high school. I'd be excited about having many options for extracurricular activities, but I wouldn't want to join any sport teams because I don't like playing sports."

Excerpt from Taesoo's Speech

"I think the level of engagement in extracurricular activities seems different between Korean and U.S. high school students. For example, many U.S. high school students tend to spend much more time doing community service than Korean students."

As seen above, Seoyeon is most likely involved in the process of ① _____, and Taesoo is most likely involved in the process of ② _____.

B

(Seoyeon and Taesoo are talking about their speeches.)

Seoyeon: I really liked your speech. There are a lot of things we can do for the community when it comes to extracurricular activities.

Taesoo : Thank you. That was the exact point I wanted to make.

Seoyeon: I'd like to hear more about the ways in which we can serve our communities.

Fill in the blanks ① and ② each with the ONE most appropriate word from <A>, in the correct order. Then, explain one of the four processes in <A> that Seoyeon in <B> is most likely involved in with evidence from <B>.

모범답안 ① reflecting ② comparing

Seoyeon in <B> engages in the process of interacting as she shares her personal meanings after learning about extracurricular activities in the U.S. and reshapes her understanding of extracurricular activities to include diverse ways to provide community services through her interaction with Taesoo.

11. Read the passage in <A> and the master plan in <B>, and follow the directions. [4 points]

A

Ms. Kim, a high school English teacher, attended an ICT workshop for English teachers. There she learned how to select digital tools that best fit her students' needs and use them appropriately. Below is the list of principles she took note of during the workshop.

<Guiding principles for using digital tools>

① *Encourage students to independently explore and discover language rules.*
② *Support learners with diverse learning styles (e.g., auditory styles, visual styles).*
③ *Teach digital ethics (e.g., citing properly).*
④ *Assess student achievement and provide individualized feedback.*

B

Draft of the Master Plan

Unit	Save the Earth	
Objectives	Students will be able to: • identify the main idea and details of a text or discourse • write an opinion using textual and non-textual elements • use digital tools responsibly and ethically	

Objectives	Contents	Technology
1st	• Introduce the topic, 'Save the Earth' • Watch a video on environmental problems • Teach how to use the Internet properly 　(e.g., locating information, sourcing, netiquette)	- Online videos - Internet search engines
2nd	• Make predictions about a text using titles and pictures • Read the passage, 'Plastic Pollution' • Identify key words and main ideas	Word cloud generator to visualize key concepts
3rd	• Provide definitions of new words • Teach grammar points explicitly using drills	PPT slides
...	...	...
7th	• Brainstorm ideas to solve environmental problems and share in groups • In groups, create a 'Save the Earth' poster	Online collaborative writing platform
8th	• Exhibit groups' posters on the walls • Conduct a team-based quiz and provide comments to groups	Online quiz platform

Based on <A>, identify the TWO guiding principles that Ms. Kim does NOT conform to in her lessons in <B>. Then, explain your answers, respectively, with evidence from <B>.

모범답안 Ms. Kim does not conform to guiding principles ① and ④. First, she explicitly teaches grammar points through drills instead of encouraging students to independently explore and discover language rules. Additionally, she conducts a team-based quiz and provides comments to groups rather than assessing individual performance and offering personalized feedback.

Contents

Theoretical Background for Classroom Teaching

Chapter 05 교수법

Chapter 06 교재 개발 및 교재 분석

Chapter 07 Differentiated Instruction

Contents

Classroom Teaching and Learning

Build Up

Chapter

01

언어 습득 및 학습 유형

Chapter 01

언어 습득 및 학습 유형

01 \ 행동주의(Behaviorism)

1 개념

(1) 학습에 대한 관점

아동은 언어와 세상에 대한 백지 상태(tabula rasa)로 태어나 환경에 의한 자극－반응－강화(stimulus－response－reinforcement)에 의해 습관화·조건화돼 언어를 습득한다. 전형적인 행동주의 이론학습은 언어적 자극에 따른 모방(imitation)과 반복(repetition)으로 올바른 반응을 이끌어 그 올바른 반응이 지속적으로 나타날 수 있도록 강화(reinforcement)함으로써 언어를 하나의 습관으로 만들고자 한다.

In behaviorism, language acquisition essentially involves habit formation in a process of **Stimulus-Response-Reinforcement**. Learners respond to the stimulus (linguistic input), and reinforcement strengthens (habituates) the response; they imitate and repeat the language that they hear, and when they are reinforced for that response, learning occurs. The implication is that "practice makes perfect."

(2) 구조주의(Structuralism)

구조주의 관점에 따르면 언어는 개별적 항목으로 분해될 수 있으며, 이런 개별 언어들은 과학적으로 기술·대조될 수 있고, 각각의 개별적 항목이 통합된 것이 바로 언어이다. 따라서 구조주의 관점을 토대로 한 교실 수업의 교수요목(syllabus)은 **structural syllabus**의 형태로 제시된다.

28　Chapter 01 언어 습득 및 학습 유형

01

In the Classroom ⫴⫴

Structural Syllabi

They focus on phonological & grammatical structures.

Chapter 1 verb tense
             1-1 the simple tenses
             1-2 the progressive tenses
             1-3 the perfect tenses
             1-4 the perfect progressive tenses
             1-5 summary chart of verb tenses
             1-6 spelling of *-ing* and *-ed* forms
Chapter 2 model auxiliaries and similar expressions
Chapter 3 the passive
Chapter 4 gerunds and infinitives

② 언어 분석 방법 – Contrastive Analysis Hypothesis

제2언어 습득을 방해하는 요인을 모국어의 간섭(**interference**)으로 보고 모국어와 L2의 차이점을 파악해 제2언어 학습에서의 어려움을 덜고자 했다. 특히 언어의 개별적 요소인 phonological and grammatical items에 있어서의 차이점에 주목한다.

Students who learn English as a foreign language already have a deep knowledge of at least one other language, and where L1 and English come into contact with each other there are often confusions which provoke errors in a learner's use of English. This can be at the level of sounds: Korean, for example, does not have a phonemic distinction between /r/ and /l/ and Korean speakers may well say ***lice*** when they mean ***rice***. It can be at the level of grammar where a student's first language has a subtly different system: our students often have trouble with article usage and the present perfect because Korean doesn't have such a form.

3 행동주의에 따른 교실 지도 – Audiolingual Method

행동주의는 프로그램 학습(programmed instruction)과 통제된 연습, 수많은 pattern drill이 사용된 청화식 교수법(audiolingual method)의 토대가 됐다. 따라서 교사는 모방과 연습, 강화 스케줄을 마련해 자신이 의도하는 방식으로 학습자가 반응하도록 학습 환경을 조성하고 반복적이고 기계적인 언어 학습을 통해 해당 언어를 습관화시키도록 한다. 즉, 문형을 반복적으로 연습시켜 외우게 한 다음, 필요에 따라 습관적으로 그 문형을 사용할 수 있도록 한다.

Materials	a dialogue / focus on lexical items and grammatical structures
Learning Method	imitation, repetition and practice / memorizing the whole dialogue / oral practice
Classroom Technique	**Drilling (pattern drilling)**: repetition, backward build-up, chain, substitution, transformation, question and answer drills
Grammar	not explicit explanation but analogy
Teacher Role	controller

▶ **Rote learning** involves the mental storage of items having little or no association with existing cognitive structure.

새로운 학습 자료는 기존 인지구조와의 상호작용 없이 개별적이고 독립적으로 단기 기억에 저장되므로 반복적인 연습이 없으면 오랫동안 기억하기 어렵다.

4 행동주의에 대한 비판

행동주의에 따르면 아동은 강화에 의해 언어를 학습한다고 주장하지만 강화를 한 번도 받지 못한 언어적 행동도 나타난다. 따라서 아동은 외부적인 환경에 의해 언어를 형성하기보다는 자신의 언어 체계를 창조적으로 발달시켜 가는 것이다. (Littlewood, 1987)

Imitation and reinforcement have a much smaller role to play in child language. For example, children often produce forms that they never heard their parents or other adults say ("I goed" or "two foots"). Thus, imitation of adult speech cannot completely account for the way children produce language: "The child's language is simply too strange (McLaughlin, 1984, p.15)." Furthermore, parents rarely correct their children's grammatical errors but respond instead to the message content (Brown and Hanlon, 1970; Brown, 1973). If ungrammatical forms are thus positively rewarded (or at least ignored), how then do children eventually eliminate them? A behaviorist view of language, which would predict the need for both imitation and negative feedback in the form of overt corrections, does not seem to explain the way in which children learn (Hadley, 2001).

02 \ 선천주의(Innatism)

1] 개념

선천주의에 따르면 아동은 언어 규칙을 이용해 언어를 구사할 수 있는 **언어 습득 장치 (Language Acquisition Device·LAD)**를 가지고 태어나기에 단기간에 언어 습득이 가능하며, 이러한 언어 습득 장치는 모든 인간에게 보편적인 것으로서 무한한 양의 창의적 발화를 도와준다.

That is, something people are born with rather than something people have learned through experience.

> ▶ innate = inherent in us, not derived from experience
> ▶ intuited/deduced = seen to be true using rational insight alone, or worked out from this insight

2] 선천주의에 따른 학습 가설 – Krashen's Input Hypothesis

An important condition for language to occur is that the acquirer understand (via hearing and reading) input language that contains structure "a bit beyond" his or her current level of competence.

Ex : If a learner is at stage 'I', then maximum acquisition takes place when he/she is exposed to "Comprehensible input" that belongs to level 'I+1.'

③ 선천주의에 따른 교실 지도 – Natural Approach

Krashen의 Input Hypothesis를 토대로 교실 수업이 진행되며, 학습 초반 자연스러운 의사소통 상황(natural communication)에서 학습자들은 교사나 언어적 능력이 뛰어난 동료 학습자로부터 다량의 이해 가능한 입력(comprehensible input)을 받음으로써 목표 언어의 이해력을 우선적으로 구축하면서 학습이 시작된다. (with perhaps more **emphasis on comprehension** than production)

As for practical ways of implementing *Natural Approach*, this will depend on the level of the class. At beginner level, lots of TPR activities are called for, where learners simply respond to instructions by performing physical actions, such as pointing at things, handing each other objects, standing, walking, sitting down, writing and drawing. At higher levels, the focus is still on providing comprehensible input, in the form of listening or reading tasks, where learners order pictures, fill in grids, follow maps, and so on.

These can be combined with communicative speaking tasks, such as 'describe-and-draw' or 'spot-the-difference,' where learners work in pairs to exchange information about pictures. The important thing is that there is no **grammar 'agenda'** as such: the learners perform the tasks to the best of their ability. New input—and hence the 'push' to improve—comes from watching the teacher or a more proficient speaker perform the same tasks.

03 \ 인지주의(Cognitivism)

1 개념

인지주의는 사람들이 어떻게 **정보**를 받아들이고 처리하는가, 주어진 정보가 어떻게 기존의 인지구조 안에 **포섭**되는가, 포섭된 정보가 어떻게 **재생**되는가에 대한 전반적인 학습 과정을 개념화하고자 한다. 즉, 인지주의는 지식 습득 과정에서의 인지적 역할 및 과정 (cognitive processing)을 설명한다.

Learning is not about the mechanics of what a learner does, but rather a process depending on what the learner already knows (existing information) and their method of acquiring new knowledge (**how they integrate new information into their existing schemata**).

2 언어 분석 방법 – Error Analysis

오류 분석은 학습자의 오류 출현을 목표어 체계에 도달하는 하나의 과정(중간언어, interlanguage)이라 인식하고 학습자의 오류를 관찰, 분석, 시정하고자 한다.

The aim of EA, first, is to identify strategies which learners use in language learning, in terms of the approaches and strategies used in both of teaching and learning. Second, to try to identify the causes of learners' errors, that is, investigating the motives behind committing such errors as the first attempt to eradicate them. Third, to obtain information on common difficulties in Language Learning, as an aid to teaching or in the preparation of the teaching materials.

3 인지주의에 따른 학습과 가설

(1) **유의미 학습**(Meaningful Learning)

인지주의는 인간의 언어 학습에는 체계성이 있기 때문에 새로운 항목을 학습했을 경우 기존 인지구조 안에 새로운 항목을 유의미하게 연관시켜 포섭한다고 설명하고 있다. 즉, 새로운 학습은 기존에 관련된 항목이 인지구조 안에 내재돼 있을 경우 더욱 효과적이며 유의미하게 학습된다는 것이다. (↔ 행동주의의 rote learning과 대조적인 학습)

01

Learning takes place in the human organism through a meaningful process of relating new events or items to already existing cognitive concepts or propositions handing new items on existing cognitive pegs. Meaningful learning is the process of relating and anchoring new material to relevant established entities in cognitive structure. As new material enters the cognitive field, it interacts with and is appropriately subsumed under, a more inclusive conceptual system. As a result, these associative links create stronger retention.

Plus ➕

유의미 학습(Meaningful Learning)

학습 과제를 기존 인지구조와 유의미하게 관련시키면서 습득하는 과정이다. 즉, 새로운 학습 과제가 인지 영역으로 들어오면 해당 학습 과제는 기존의 인지구조와의 상호작용을 통해 보다 포괄적인 인지구조 속으로 포섭된다. 따라서 유의미 학습은 장기 기억에 유리하다.

It subsumes new information into existing structures and memory systems and the resulting associative links create stronger retention.

> ▶ **Advance Organizer**
>
> 학습자들이 가지고 있는 기존의 지식과 관련된 정보를 제시함으로써, 학습자가 기존 지식을 회상하고 새로운 정보에 적용해 새로운 지식을 의미 있게 조직하고 해석할 수 있도록 유도한다.
>
> Using an Advance Organizer, the teacher begins by giving the students a general orientation to the activities to come. To assist comprehension, this introduction may be given in the students' L1. Use of an Advance Organizer is believed to activate the students' previously developed knowledge for top-down processing, and assist them in linking the new information to what they already know.
>
> ▶ **기계적 학습(Rote Learning)**
>
> 기존의 인지구조와 유의미한 관련 없이 학습 과제를 각기 독립된 개별 항목으로 습득하는 과정이다.
>
> Taking in isolated bits and pieces of information that are not connected with one's existing cognitive structures.

(2) Information Processing Model

언어 형태의 관심 정도에 따라 집중적인(**focal**) 관심과 부수적인(**peripheral**) 관심으로, 정보처리 단계에 따라 일시적인 능력인 통제된 정보처리 능력(**controlled processing**)과 영구적인 능력인 자동화된 처리 능력(**automatic processing**)으로 분류하고 있다.

① Controlled processing: 학습 상황에서 얻게 된 지식을 제한적/의식적으로 처리

② Automatic processing: 학습 상황에서 얻게 된 지식을 자동적/무의식적으로 처리

(3) Implicit and Explicit Knowledge Model

제2언어 학습에서 얻게 된 지식을 묵시적 지식(implicit knowledge)과 명시적 지식 (explicit knowledge)으로 나눠 외국어 학습 과정을 설명하고 있다. 이때, 명시적 지식은 교실 수업에서 유의미한 연습(meaningful practice)을 통해 습득과 유사한 개념인 묵시적 지식으로 전환될 수 있다고 한다.

① Explicit linguistic knowledge: 교실 수업을 통해 얻어진 언어에 관한 지식으로 언어의 표면적인 특징과 규칙을 설명할 수 있는 지식

② Implicit linguistic knowledge: 자연스러운 의사소통 상황을 통해 얻어진 지식으로 언어 사용 시 자동적으로 재생되는 지식

4 인지주의에 따른 교실 지도 – Form–Focused Instruction

'Focus on form' and **'focus on forms'** refer to differing instructional practices in the second language classroom. Instructional methods with aspects of both types of instruction include consciousness raising activities and input based instruction.

(1) Focus on Form

It consists of primarily meaning-focused interaction in which there is brief, and sometimes spontaneous, attention to linguistic forms. Focus on form assumes that acquisition occurs best when learners' attention is drawn to language items when they are needed for communication. Types of focus on form include **input flood, input enhancement, and corrective feedback**.

(2) Focus on Forms

It involves a primary emphasis on linguistic structures, often presented as **discrete grammar rules** or other **metalinguistic information**. Focus on forms emphasizes **the role of explicit knowledge** in the acquisition process. Types of focus on forms include present, practice, produce (**PPP**) and explicit language instruction (**garden path**).

04 \ 구성주의(Constructivism)

1 개념

(1) 구성주의

인지주의와 분리된 이론을 펼치는 것이 아니라, 구성주의 관점에서 언어의 본질적인 면을 사회적 맥락 안에서 사회적 상호작용을 토대로 더욱 심층적으로 연구하는 이론이다. 또한 자신에게 주어지는 지식을 수동적으로 받아들이는 것이 아니라, 사회적 상호작용을 통해 지식을 능동적으로 재구성한다.

Constructivism is a theory of learning that claims that individuals actively construct knowledge, rather than passively receiving it. They do this by filtering and organizing their experiences so as to match their existing knowledge (or mental representations) of the world. If there is a mismatch between their experiences and their existing mental representations, they restructure the latter to accommodate the new information. According to this view, different individuals who are exposed to the same experiences will each construct a different and unique reality.

(2) 기능주의

언어에는 기능적인(**function**) 측면이 존재하는데, 이는 사회적 맥락(**social context**) 안에서 달라진다. 따라서 언어 자체의 기능적인 측면을 고려해 사회적 상호작용 속에서 구현되는 언어의 기능을 학습해야 한다.

① Language is a system for the expression of **meaning**.
② The primary function of language is **for interaction and communication**.
③ The structure of language reflects its **functional communicative uses**.
④ The primary units of language are not merely its grammatical and structural features but categories of functional and communicative meaning as exemplified in **discourse**.

즉, 기능주의에 따르면 언어는 의미를 나타내기 위한 체계이므로 자연스러운 상황에서의 언어 사용 기회를 제공하고, 즉각적인 피드백과 즉흥적인 언어 사용을 중시하며, 단일 언어능력의 학습보다 실제 생활과 유사한 상황이 중심이 된 **통합적인 수업 모형**을 추구 한다.

 In the Classroom

Functional Syllabus

This type of syllabus contains a collection of the functions that are performed when language is used. It includes: informing, agreeing, apologizing, requesting, promising, and so on. Examples of notions include size, age, color, comparison, time, etc.

Function	Apologizing	Requesting directions	Expressing frustration
Situation	Department store	At the bus stop	Home (Dinner guests late)
Communicative Expressions	I'm sorry! Would it be possible...?	I beg your pardon? / Could you tell me...?	How inconsiderate! Why couldn't they have telephoned?
Structure	Simple past / Present perfect	Interrogative (simple present) / Modal-must	Be+verb / It's (time)

2 언어 분석 방법 – Discourse Analysis

담화란 글의 흐름 및 연속체를 뜻하는데, 담화 분석은 문장 간의 관계를 연구해 글의 **결합력(cohesion)**과 **일관성(coherence)**을 토대로 글의 통일성(unified text)을 연구하고자 한다. 따라서 구성주의 교실 수업은 기능에 초점을 두고 학습이 이뤄진다. 기능이란 문장 안(sentence level)이 아니라 문장과 문장 간(suprasentential level or discourse level) 담화에 존재하므로, 구성주의 학습은 담화상에서 사용된 언어 형식과 기능 간의 관계를 통해 언어가 사용되는 상황과 언어를 분석하고자 한다.

③ 기능주의 및 구성주의에 따른 학습

기능주의 및 구성주의에 따른 언어 학습은 언어의 본질적인 요소인 언어의 기능을 중시하므로, 실제 교실 지도에서 언어의 기능 학습이라는 대명제로 학습자 중심의 언어 학습을 시도했다.

(1) Schematic Knowledge

Language learners make use of their knowledge of the world to help them comprehend texts. Research has shown that learners possess **schemata**, i.e., mental structures that organize their knowledge of the world which they draw on in interpreting what they heard or read.

(2) Individual Difference

If some people are better at some things than others—better at analysing, for example—this would indicate that there are differences in the ways individual brains work. It also suggests that people respond differently to the same stimuli. If we accept that different intelligences predominate in different people, it suggests that the same learning task may not be appropriate for all of our students.

Plus ➕

Multiple Intelligences

Howard Gardner proposed that individuals have "multiple intelligences" and that traditional IQ tests have assessed only a limited range of abilities. Among the "multiple intelligences" Gardner includes abilities in the areas of music, interpersonal relations, and athletics, as well as the verbal intelligence that is most often associated with success in school.

	Meaning	Examples
Logical/ Mathematical	the ability to use numbers effectively, to see abstract patterns, and to reason well	puzzles and games, logical, sequential presentations, classifications and categorizations
Visual/ Spatial	the ability to orient oneself in the environment, to create mental images, and a sensitivity to shape, size, color	charts and grids, videos, drawing
Body/ Kinesthetic	the ability to use one's body to express oneself and to solve problems	hands-on-activities, field trips, pantomime
Musical/ Rhythmic	the ability to recognize tonal patterns and a sensitivity to rhythm, pitch, melody	singing, playing music, jazz chants
Interpersonal	the ability to understand another person's moods, feelings, motivations, and intentions	pairwork, project work, group problem-solving
Intrapersonal	the ability to understand one self and to practice self-discipline	self-evaluation, journal keeping, options for homework
Verbal/ Linguistic	the ability to use language effectively and creatively	note-taking, story telling, debates

(3) Personalization

학습 활동 중 학생들이 자신의 생각과 감정 및 선호하는 것을 토대로 언어를 표현하고 사용하도록 함으로써 실제적 의사소통 학습이 가능하며 교실 수업을 보다 활동적이고 역동적으로 진행할 수 있다.

When you personalize language you use it to talk about your knowledge, experience and feelings. Personalization creates better classroom dynamics. Thus, personalization happens when activities allow students to use language to express their own ideas, feelings, preferences and opinions. Also, it is an important part of the communicative approach, since it involves true communication, as learners communicate real information about themselves.

Ex ┃ The learners have read a text about sports. In pairs they talk about what their favourite sports are and whether they prefer to play or watch.

In the classroom, personalization is important for several reasons. It makes language relevant to learners, makes communication activities meaningful, and also helps memorization. Personalization can take place at any stage of a lesson.

(4) Learner-centered Instruction

2015년 교육과정 개정에 따른 현 교실 수업의 대표적인 수업 모델인 Learner-centered Instruction은 기존의 교사 위주의 수업 방식보다 학생들의 적극적인 참여로 학생들이 주체가 돼 교실 활동 전반을 이끌어 나가고자 한다.

Learner-centered instruction aims to give learners more say in areas that are traditionally considered the domain of the teacher by providing learners with greater autonomy. This term applies to curricular as well as to specific techniques. It can be contrasted with teacher-centered, and has received various recent interpretations. Learner-centered instruction includes :

① techniques that focus on or account for learners' needs, styles, and goals
② techniques that give some control to the student (group work or strategy training, for example)

③ curricula that include the consultation and input of students and that do not presuppose objectives in advance

④ techniques that allow for student creativity and innovation

⑤ techniques that enhance a student's sense of competence and self-worth

> ▶ Flipped learning：혼합형 학습의 한 형태로, 수업에서 정보기술을 활용해 학습을 극대화할 수 있도록 강의보다는 학생과의 상호작용에 수업 시간을 더 할애하는 교수 학습 방식을 말한다. 흔히 적용되는 방식으로는 교사가 준비한 수업 영상과 자료를 학생이 수업 시간 전에 미리 보고 학습하는 형태가 있다. 그 후 교실 수업 시간에 교사는 교과 내용을 중심으로 가르치는 대신 학생들과 상호작용하거나 심화 학습 활동을 하는 데 더 많은 시간을 할애할 수 있다.

⑸ Integrated Approach

실제 생활(real life) 안에서의 언어 사용은 개별적인 언어능력, 즉 듣기, 말하기, 읽기, 쓰기 등이 독립적으로 사용되는 것이 아니다. 따라서 통합적인 측면에서 실제 효과적인 언어 학습을 이뤄야 적절한 의사소통 능력을 배양할 수 있다. 이러한 목적을 실현하기 위해 whole language approach 측면에서 통합 수업 모형(integrated approach), 즉 듣기, 말하기, 읽기, 쓰기 등의 수업 연계가 현재 교실 수업에서 실현되고 있는 것이다.

Integrated skills activities can provide a model for integrating skills in a realistic way and is especially useful at a post-elementary level. Another simple but effective way of ensuring that skills are integrated is to get the learners to collaborate, in pairs or in groups, on many of the fluency-focused tasks described. Finally, both simulation and project work provide a natural framework for integrating skills. Project work is described below. First, however, we need to see why integrated skills activities are important：

① They provide opportunities for using language naturally, not just practising it.

② Many pair-and group activities call for a variety of skills, sometimes simultaneously, in order to involve all the learners.

③ Students seem to learn better when they are engaged in activities which involve more than one skill.

4 구성주의에 따른 교실 지도 – Communicative Language Teaching

의사소통 교수는 교실 수업에서 언어의 형태보다 기능에 초점을 두고 다량의 상호작용 및 의사소통을 촉진하는 수업 모형이며, 실제 자료(authentic texts)를 기반으로 한 통합 수업(integrated skills use)을 지향한다.

The purpose of Communicative Language Teaching is to help students produce authentic language and communicate with others. To produce authentic language does not mean developing speaking skills only. CLT integrates multiple skills, such as listening and writing. To help students communicate, the teacher need to provide rich and authentic input.

There can be many approaches to achieve Communicative Language Teaching. Task-based teaching is the most common teaching approach. Teachers set up a goal, give students real-life language tasks, and students respond in a meaning way. In this process, students are motivated to use the language to serve the purpose of communication.

In CLT, meaning exceeds forms, but it does not mean that grammar is not important. Teachers should teach grammar within contexts and through communicative tasks. In this way, grammar is not presented as a list of rigid rules, but natural patterns that students acquire in the learning contexts.

Chapter
02

제2언어 습득 모형

제2언어 습득 모형

01 선천주의 모형

1 Krashen의 Input Hypothesis

Krashen의 Input Hypothesis는 이해 가능한 입력 자료(**comprehensible input**, **_i+1_**)를 언어 습득의 가장 중요한 요소로 보고 자연스러운 의사소통 상황을 통해 언어를 습득하게 된다고 봤다. 즉, 이 가설은 원어 수업(English ONLY classroom) 필요성의 이론적 토대가 돼왔다.

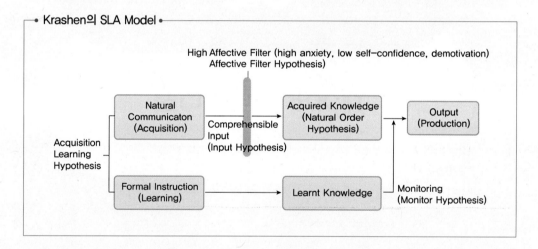

Krashen의 SLA Model

(1) 학습 이론-습득-학습 가설(Acquisition-Learning Hypothesis)

외국어 학습 과정은 모국어의 학습 과정과 동일한 자연스러운 의사소통 방식(**natural communication**)과 문법 학습의 형식적 교수 방식(**formal instruction**)으로 진행되는데, 이때 보다 성공적인 외국어 학습을 위해서는 자연스러운 의사소통 방식의 acquisition 과정으로 진행돼야 한다.

Acquisition occurs subconsciously as a result of participating in natural communication where the focus is on meaning. **Learning**, which refers to conscious processes that result in explicit knowledge about the grammar properties of a second language. Thus, acquired knowledge serves as the major source for initiating both the comprehension and production of utterances. Learnt knowledge is available for use only by the monitor. Learning cannot lead to acquisition(non-interface position).

(2) **학습 조건** – Input Hypothesis and Affective Filter Hypothesis

① **Input Hypothesis**: 언어 습득은 학습자의 현재 수준보다 한 단계 높은 입력 자료 (comprehensible input, $i+1$)가 제공될 경우 일어난다. 언어적 입력 자료는 학습자의 배경지식과 상황, 몸짓(gesture), 억양 등으로 학습자에게 이해 가능하도록 제시될 수 있다. 이러한 입력 자료가 제공된 후 학습자는 침묵기(silent period)를 거쳐 발화를 하게 된다.

According to the Input Hypothesis, the learners improve and progress along the "natural order" when they receive comprehensible input. Comprehensible input is defined as second language input just beyond the learner's current second language competence, in terms of its syntactic complexity. If a learner's current competence is i then **comprehensible input is i+1**, the next step in the developmental sequence. Input which is either too simple (already acquired) or too complex ($i+2/3$...) will not be useful for acquisition. Krashen views the Input Hypothesis as central to his model of second language acquisition.

Plus ⊕

The Requirement of Optimal Input

1. 이해 가능해야 한다. (comprehensible)
2. 흥미롭고 서로 관련된 자료여야 한다. (interesting and relevant)
3. 문법적인 순서로 제시할 필요는 없다. (not grammatically sequenced)
4. 학습자의 수준보다 한 단계 높게 제시돼야 한다. (supplied as $i+1$)
5. 학습자의 정의적 측면을 고려한 학습 환경을 제시해야 한다. (delivered in an environment where students are "off the defensive")

② **Affective Filter Hypothesis**: 정의적 여과막이란 학습자가 지닌 학습에 대한 정의적인 변인이 학습에 장애가 되는 방향으로 작용하는 것을 말하며, 낮은 동기 및 자신감, 높은 불안감 등을 예로 들 수 있다. 따라서 성공적인 언어 습득을 위해서는 이러한 정의적 여과막이 낮아야 한다.

The affective filter is "a mental block" that prevents acquirers from fully utilizing the comprehensible input they receive for language acquisition. A number of affective variables such as motivation, self-esteem and low anxiety can play a facilitative role in successful second language acquisition. Low motivation, low self-esteem, and high anxiety, on the other hand, can work to raise an affective filter. In other words, when the filter is up it hinders language acquisition.

(3) Natural Order Hypothesis

문법 체계는 예측 가능한 순서대로 습득되는데, 이러한 자연적인 발달 순서는 문법 구조의 복잡성이나 의도적인 문법 지도와는 별개로 발달한다.

The natural order hypothesis states that the acquisition of grammatical structures in a second language follows a predictable natural order. This order is independent of instructional sequences or even of the complexity of the structures to be acquired. Thus, when the learners are engaged in natural communication tasks they will manifest the standard order.

Plus ➕

Morpheme Order Study

아동들의 문법적 형태소 습득 순서에 관한 연구에서 학습자의 언어 습득은 학습자의 나이나 모국어와 관계없이 일정한 순서의 양상을 보인다는 것이 밝혀지면서 대조 분석에 대한 비판에 힘이 실렸다.

Researchers found that a consistent order of emergence (natural order of acquisition) of grammatical morphemes (for example, plural −s, past tense −ed, and articles) that was not influenced by the learner's age or first language in their study of children acquiring English as a second language.

(4) Monitor Hypothesis

모니터란 학습자의 발화에서 오류를 감지해 잘못된 표현을 개선하거나 수정하는 장치이다. Krashen에 따르면 학습된 언어적 지식(learnt knowledge)이 학습자의 언어 출력을 감시하는 모니터 역할을 수행한다.

Learning has only one function, and that is as a monitor or editor to make changes in the form of our utterance, after it has been produced by the acquired system. Acquisition initiates the speaker's utterances and is responsible for fluency. Thus, the monitor is thought to alter the output of the acquired system before or after the utterance is actually written or spoken.

> **Plus ➕**
>
> 성공적인 모니터를 위한 조건
>
> 1. 학습된 규칙을 선택하고 적용하기 위한 충분한 시간이 있어야 한다.
>   There must be sufficient time.
>
> 2. 언어 출력의 정확성과 형태에 초점을 맞춰야 한다.
>   The focus must be on form and not meaning.
>
> 3. 출력된 언어에 적용된 규칙을 알아야 한다.
>   The user must know the rule.

2 시사점

(1) 교실 적용

① The main function of the classroom may be to provide comprehensible input in an environment conducive to a low affective filter (i.e., high motivation, low anxiety).

② Error correction should be minimal in the classroom; it is of some limited use when the goal is learning, but of no use when the goal is acquisition. Error correction raises the affective filter and should, therefore, not be used in free conversation or when acquisition is likely to take place.

③ Students should never be required to produce speech in the second language unless they are ready to do so. Speaking fluency cannot be taught, but "emerges" naturally in time with enough comprehensible input. (Hadley, 2001)

(2) Krashen 모형에 대한 비판

① Acquisition-Learning Hypothesis에 대한 비판: 학습된 언어적 지식은 연습을 통해 습득으로 이어질 수 있다.

② 학습자의 능동적인 참여 간과: 학습자의 노력과 전략에 따라 교사나 다른 학습자로부터 많은 입력을 유발하는 학습자(HIGs)가 수동적인 학습자(LIGs)보다 상대적으로 더 많은 학습 효과를 보인다.

③ 지속적인 침묵기: 일정 기간 동안 이해 가능한 입력을 받았음에도 불구하고 침묵기(**silent period**)에 머무르는 학습자에 대해 설명하지 못한다.

④ Output의 중요성 간과: Krashen은 제2언어 습득의 유일한 요인으로 이해 가능한 입력($i+1$)을 강조했지만, 실제 제2언어 습득에서는 입력(input)만큼이나 출력(output)도 중요하다.

⑤ 학습자에게 제공되는 모든 입력이 흡수(intake)로 이어지지 않는다.

Plus ➕

1. Swain's Output Hypothesis : Pushed Output

Swain preferred to take a stronger stand for the importance of the role of output in her development of the Output Hypothesis. She argued that among other functions, output is a significant way to test out hypotheses about the target language. Swain (1995) suggests that "**pushed output**" (i.e., output that is accurate and sociolinguistically appropriate) may be necessary for learners to achieve higher levels of linguistic and sociolinguistic competence. According to Swain (1995), pushed output facilitates acquisitions, as it ① helps learners to discover that there is a gap between what they want to say and what they are able to say, ② provides a way for learners to try out new rules and modify them accordingly, and ③ helps learners to actively reflect on what they know about the target language system. According to Ellis (1997), learners "need to see for themselves what has gone wrong, in the operating conditions under which they went wrong."

> Ex | A: I go cinema.
> B: You what?
> A: I went to the cinema.

In the example, A is led to reformulate her initial utterance, producing a more grammatical version of it, as a result of B's clarification request. Thus, this kind of exchange provides an opportunity for what Swain has called ***pushed output***, i.e., output that reflects what learners can produce when they are pushed to use the target language accurately and concisely.

2. The Role of Output in SLA

① to notice their erroneous attempts to convey meaning

② to recognize linguistic shortcomings

③ to try out one's language to test various hypotheses that are forming

02 \ 인지주의 모형

1 McLaughlin의 Information Processing Model

정보처리 모형은 제2언어 학습을 해당 언어의 인지적인 처리 과정으로 본다. 언어적인 정보는 통제된 처리 과정을 거쳐 자동화된 처리 과정에 도달하게 된다. McLaughlin은 학습자의 언어 사용 범주에 따라 외국어 학습을 4개 범주로 분류하고 있다. 즉 언어 형태의 관심 정도에 따라 집중적인(focal) 관심과 부수적인(peripheral) 관심으로, 정보처리 단계에 따라 일시적인 능력인 통제된 정보처리 능력(controlled processing)과 영구적인 능력인 자동화된 처리 능력(automatic processing)으로 분류하고 있다.

(1) **언어 형태에 대한 집중도**(Attention to Formal Properties of Language)

① **Focal**: 언어 형식에 집중적인 관심을 보인다.

② **Peripheral**: 언어 형식에 부수적인 관심을 보인다.

(2) **정보처리 과정**(Information Processing)

① **Controlled processing**: 형식적인 수업에 의해 처음 학습 자료가 제시됐을 경우, 일시적으로 갖게 되는 언어능력에 의한 정보처리 과정이다(learning).

② **Automatic processing**: 연습에 의해 일상적인 언어능력이 돼 무의식적인 과정을 통해 이뤄지는 정보처리 과정이다(acquisition).

Controlled processing demands a lot of attentional control on the part of the subjects and it is constrained by the limitations of the short-term memory. Through practice, sequences first produced by controlled processing become automatic. Automatized sequences are stored as units in the long-term memory, which means that they can be made available very rapidly whenever the situation requires it, with minimal attentional control on the part of the subject.

(3) 자동적 정보처리 능력 과정

학습자는 초기 학습 자료 제시에 의해 한정된 언어능력으로 정보처리 과정을 겪으나, 유의미한 연습(meaningful practice)을 통해 영구적인 정보처리 과정으로 이동할 수 있다. 또한 이런 지식들은 재구조화 과정을 통해 장기 기억에 내재화된다.

According to cognitive theory, second-language learning, like any other complex cognitive skill, involves the gradual integration of subskills as controlled process initially predominate and then become automatic. Thus the initial stage of learning involves the slow development of skills and the gradual elimination of errors as the learner attempts to automatize aspects of performance. In later phases, there is continual restructuring as learners shift their internal representations.

2 Bialystok의 Implicit and Explicit Model

Bialystok은 Krashen이 주장한 '습득과 학습'과 유사한 개념인 묵시적 지식(암시적 지식, implicit knowledge)과 명시적 지식(explicit knowledge)을 토대로 외국어 과정을 설명했는데, 명시적 지식은 연습을 통해 습득과 유사한 개념인 묵시적 지식으로 전환될 수 있다고 한다(interface position).

Explicit and implicit knowledge are not unrelated to the distinction between declarative and procedural knowledge. **Declarative knowledge** can be based on explicit knowledge and **procedural knowledge** underlies implicit knowledge. The difference, however, is that in the case of explicit knowledge, awareness is a key issue. Through practice and exposure, explicit knowledge can become implicit and vice versa.

(1) 명시적 언어 지식(Explicit Knowledge)

언어에 관한 지식으로 언어의 형태나 표면적인 특징에 대해 설명할 수 있는 지식이다.

Knowledge to know about language and the ability to articulate those facts in some way

(2) 묵시적 언어 지식(암시적 지식, Implicit Knowledge)

유의미적 학습에서 생기는 것으로 언어 수행에서 자동적으로 사용되는 지식이다.

Information that is automatically and spontaneously used in language tasks

---

Further Reading

1. Declarative Knowledge & Procedural Knowledge

Declarative knowledge is concerned with knowledge "about something" (knowing that). With regard to language, it relates to such aspects of language as word knowledge (collocation, pronunciation, meaning). This information is relatively accessible to conscious awareness. Procedural knowledge relates to cognitive skills (know how). Using language is thought to involve procedural knowledge and, unlike declarative knowledge, is relatively inaccessible.

2. Noticing Hypothesis

According to noticing hypothesis, nothing is learned unless it has been noticed. Noticing does not itself result in acquisition, but it is the essential starting point. Noticing refers to becoming aware of a language feature in the input.

> ▶ **Noticing the Gap Principle**
>
> According to Noticing the Gap Principle, attention to (language) input is a conscious process. It is said that NOTICING (registering formal features in the input) and NOTICING THE GAP (identifying how the input to which the learner is exposed to differs from the output the learner is able to generate) are as essential processes in second language acquisition. That is, 'Noticing the gap' happens when learners focus on the gaps in their own linguistic knowledge. This may happen when students do a dictogloss — sometimes referred to as grammar dictation.

Further Reading

선천주의 모델과 인지주의 모델을 통한 외국어 학습에 있어 형식적인 교수(formal instruction) 역할의 3가지 입장

1. Krashen의 모형(비접촉적 입장, Non-interface Position)

Krashen은 언어 형태에 초점을 둔 형식적인 외국어 학습에서 얻어진 학습된 지식은 습득으로 이어지지 않는다고 하면서 습득된 지식과 학습된 지식은 완전히 분리된 지식으로서 서로 관련이 없다고 본다. Krashen에 의하면 외국어 교실의 가치는 문법 교수에 있는 것이 아니라 이해 가능한 교사의 언어(teacher talk)에 있으며, 외국어 교수가 언어 형태보다 의사소통에 초점을 둘 때 진정한 의미의 습득이 일어난다는 것이다.

2. McLaughlin과 Bialystok의 모형(접촉적 입장, Interface Position)

McLaughlin은 학습자가 비록 다양한 종류의 외국어 지식을 갖고 있지만, 이 지식은 서로 분리된 것이 아니라 연습을 통해 어느 한 지식이 다른 쪽으로 바뀔 수 있다고 본다. Bialystok에 의하면 명시적 지식은 연습을 통해 습득과 유사한 암시적(묵시적) 지식으로 전환될 수 있다. 또한 교실에서 외국어를 배운 학습자는 자연적인 외국어 학습자를 능가한다고 봤는데, 그 이유는 첫째, 직접적으로는 흡입(intake)이 가능한 교실 환경 때문이며, 둘째, 간접적으로는 연습을 통해 명시적 지식을 자동화시킬 수 있기 때문이다.

03 \ 구성주의 모형

1 Long의 Interaction Hypothesis

언어 습득에 기여하는 **상호작용(interaction)**의 기능을 강조한다. 언어의 습득은 상호작용 과정 중에 발생하는 의미의 협상(negotiation of meaning)과 수정된 상호작용 (modified interaction)에 의해 언어적 입력이 더욱 이해 가능해진다는 것이다. Long의 Interaction Hypothesis는 현재 의사소통 중심 언어 수업(communicative language teaching)을 기반으로 하는 교실 수업을 뒷받침한다.

Plus ➕

1. Modified Interaction과 언어 습득의 관계

① Interaction modification makes input comprehensible.

② Comprehensible input promotes acquisition.

③ Therefore, interaction modification promotes acquisition.

2. The Role of Interaction in the Classroom

① Negotiation of meaning을 유발한다.

② Comprehensible input을 보다 많이 접할 수 있게 한다.

③ Comprehensible output의 재생을 돕는다.

④ 자신의 언어 규칙을 검증하는 기회를 제공한다.

⑤ 상황에 따른 제2언어 사용의 기회를 제공한다.

---

(1) **초기 입장** – Importance of Comprehensible Input

Krashen의 comprehensible input이 언어 습득에서 반드시 필요하다고 언급하고 있으나, comprehensible input을 제공하는 방식은 실제 학습자의 현재 상태를 분명히 파악할 수 있는 교실 내 상호작용 안에서 가능하며, 교사가 제공하는 언어적 입력이 이해 가능하지 않을 경우(incomprehesible) 의미의 협상(negotiation of meaning)을 위한 수정된 상호 작용을 통해 보다 이해 가능한 입력(comprehensible input)을 제공할 수 있다고 주장하고 있다.

According to Interaction Hypothesis, conversational interaction is an essential for second language acquisition. Long agreed with Krashen that comprehensible input is necessary for language acquisition but argued that modification of the interactional structure of conversation is a better candidate for a necessary (not sufficient) condition for acquisition. The role which plays in negotiation for meaning helps to make input comprehensible while still containing unknown linguistic elements, and, hence, potential intake for acquisition.

> Ex   Teacher   : Did you get high marks?
> Student 1 : *High marks?*
> Teacher   : Did you get *good grades?* I mean A's and B's—did you get A in English?
> Student 1 : Oh no, in English, yes em B.

(2) 후기 입장 – Importance of Corrective Feedback

의사소통 가설의 후기 입장은 의사소통 과정에서 일어나는 교정적인 정보(corrective feedback)의 중요성을 강조했다. 대화 참여자들은 의미의 협상 과정을 통해 의사소통의 어려움을 해결할 뿐 아니라 언어를 발달시킬 수 있는 기회를 얻는다고 본다.

In Long's (1996) revised version of the Interaction Hypothesis, more emphasis is placed on the importance of corrective feedback during interaction. When communication is difficult, interlocutors must "negotiate for meaning" and this negotiation is seen as the opportunity for language development. Merrill Swain (1985) extended this thinking when she proposed "the comprehensible output hypothesis." She observed that it is when learners must produce language that their interlocutor can understand that they are most likely to see the limits of their second language ability and the need to find better ways to express their meaning. The demands of producing comprehensible output, she hypothesized, "push" learners ahead in their development.

> Ex   Teacher   : How old are you?
> Student 2 : Thirteen.
> Teacher   : *Pardon me?*
> Student 2 : Thirty.

2 Modification

(1) Input Modification

학습자의 이해를 돕기 위해 담화자가 자신이 제공하는 입력을 단순하게 하는 것으로, 보다 쉬운 어휘와 명확한 발음, 단문 사용 및 비언어적 상황 등이 이에 해당한다.

Vocabulary	• use of more common vocabulary • avoidance of idioms ; lexical modification • use of nouns rather than pronouns
Grammar	• shorter utterances • less complex utterances ; syntactic modification • more regular surface structure • increased use of present tense
Pronunciation	• slower speech • clear articulation • more frequent use of standard forms • less vowel-reduction • greater stress differentiation • wider pitch range • more pauses/longer pauses
Non-verbal	• increased use of gesture • increased use of facial expression

(2) Interaction Modification – Negotiation Strategies

학습자의 이해를 돕기 위해 학습자와의 상호작용 중 대화의 구조를 조정함으로써 입력을 이해 가능하게 만드는 경우이다.

① **Confirmation checks**: 앞선 발화에 대해서 청자가 자신의 이해의 정도를 확인하는 경우

One speaker seeks confirmation of the other's preceding utterance through repetition, with rising-intonation, of what was perceived to be all or part of the preceding utterance.

Ex You mean...?

② **Comprehension checks**: 발화자가 자신의 발화에 대한 청자의 이해 여부를 확인하는 경우

One speaker attempts to determine whether the other speaker has understood a preceding message.

> Ex : Do you understand?

③ **Clarification requests**: 앞선 발화에 대해서 청자가 추가적인 설명이나 정보를 요구하는 경우

One speaker seeks assistance in understanding the other speaker's preceding utterance through questions, statements or imperatives.

> Ex : Pardon?

 In the Classroom

Exercise 1

NS : And right on the roof of the truck place the duck.
NNS : ⓐ Dog?
NS : Duck. It is yellow and has two feet. Quack, quack. ⓑ OK?
NNS : Oh, I see. ⓒ I put where it?
NS : Put it on the top of the truck.

Exercise 2

T : ... what other advantages do you think you may have, if you were the only child in the family?
S : I'm sorry. ⓓ I beg your pardon?
T : Er, if you were the only child in your family, then what other advantages you may have? What points, what other good points you may have?
S : It's quieter for my study.
T : Yes? ⓔ It's quieter for you to study. Yes? Any other?
S : No more.
T : OK. Fine.

Exercise 3

A : I was really chuffed.

B : ⓕ <u>Uh?</u>

A : Really pleased.

Exercise 4

A : I was really chuffed?

B : ⓖ <u>You were pleased?</u>

A : Yes.

Exercise 5

A : I go to cinema at weekend.

B : ⓗ <u>You went to the cinema.</u> What did you see?

A : "Gladiators." It was great.

➡ ⓐ confirmation check   ⓑ comprehension check
    ⓒ clarification request   ⓓ clarification request
    ⓔ confirmation check   ⓕ clarification request
    ⓖ confirmation check   ⓗ recast

 In the Classroom

Lexical and Syntactic Modification

<u>Linguistic modification</u> is a common occurrence in second language communication, as demonstrated in almost any case of a native English speaker interacting with a beginning English learner. <u>Slow rate of speaking, emphasis of key words, use of common vocabulary, and repetition</u> are all modifications to aid comprehension. These adaptations are all ways that an English learner's negotiation of language can be facilitated, and they are performed almost instinctively by native speakers.

02

Spoken language can be negotiated between the speaker and receiver as the language is generated, and the speaker can adapt the message according to their perception of the receiver's understanding and proficiency. However, for readers in a second language, the written input cannot be negotiated in the same way that oral input can be. In short, for negotiation to occur, the material must be adapted before it is received by the language learner (Hatch, 1983). This idea of adaptation or modification often conflicts with the notion of "authentic" input. However, because interaction between writer and reader is largely one-sided, with negotiation of the message depending on the reader's ability to correctly interpret and process the writer's message, pre-reading modifications are crucial in aiding comprehension.

The other option for finding linguistically appropriate texts, then, is to change the composition of existing texts so that they are more accessible to the L2 learner. This approach is often referred to as **simplification**. It is defined that simplification as "selection of a restricted set of features form the full range of language resources for the sake of pedagogic efficiency."

1. Low frequent words are changed into high frequent words or added with linguistic information.

① Original sentence: The Just Society seems to have *sprouted* among other founding principles.

② Simplified treatment: The Just Society seems to have *grown* among other founding principles.

③ Elaborated treatment: The Just Society seems to have *sprouted (started to grow)* among other founding principles.

2. Complex sentences were shortened.

① Original sentence: Bills of rights, which were very popular in the eighteenth century, had been *affixed* to several state constitutions and promulgated elsewhere as well.

② Modified sentence: Bills of rights had been *attached* to several state constitutions.

3 Vygotsky의 Sociocultural Theory

Long과 마찬가지로 언어 습득에서 상호작용의 역할을 중시하면서 상호작용이 언어 습득에 끼치는 영향을 근접발달영역(**The Zone of Proximal Development**)과 비계 (**scaffolding**) 등의 개념으로 설명한다.

A key concept in Sociocultural Theory is that interaction not only facilitates language learning but is a causative force in acquisition; further, all of learning is seen as essentially a social process which is grounded in sociocultural settings.

(1) 근접발달영역(The Zone of Proximal Development)

학습자가 혼자서는 해결할 수 없지만 자신보다 뛰어난 동료 혹은 성인의 도움으로는 해 결할 수 있는 잠재적인 학습 영역을 뜻한다.

The distance between the actual developmental level as determined by independent problem solving and the level of potential development as determined through problem solving under adult guidance or in collaboration with more capable peers. What this means is that learning results from interpersonal activity.

(2) Scaffolding Hypothesis

비계(**scaffolding**)는 더 뛰어난 학습자 혹은 성인이 의사소통 과정에서 학습자에게 제 공하는 도움을 뜻한다. 이는 학습자에게 언어적 입력을 더욱 이해 가능하게 만들어 의사 소통의 문제를 해결할 뿐만 아니라 ZPD 내에서의 언어 발달을 촉진하는 기능을 한다.

One way in which others help the learner in language development within the ZPD is through **scaffolding**. This includes the *vertical constructions*, in which experts commonly provide learners with chunks of talk that the learners can then use to express concepts which are beyond their independent means. More generally, the metaphor of scaffolding refers to *verbal guidance* which an expert provides to help a learner perform any specific task, or the verbal collaboration of peers to perform a task which would be too difficult for any one of them individually.

In the Classroom

1. Collaborative Dialogue (Scaffolding)

The following constructed dialogue illustrates the negotiation of meaning in a typical one-to-one communication. In this kind of collaboration, the "stretching" to higher levels of development become more obvious.

S : I throw it-box. (*He points to a box on the floor.*)
T : You *threw* the box.
S : No, I threw in the box.
T : *What did you throw in the box?*
S : My... I... paint...
T : Your *painting?*
S : Painting?
T : You know... painting. (*The teacher makes painting movements on an imaginary paper.*)
S : Yes, painting.
T : You threw your painting in the box.
S : Yes, *I threw my painting in box.*

The teacher's input is near the student's *i+1*. It provides **scaffolds** upon which the student can build. The conversation is about the immediate environment, the vocabulary is simple, repetitions are frequent, and acting out is used.

2. Jigsaw Classroom: Listening or Reading Activity

A jigsaw listening or reading activity is an *information gap exercise*. Learners hear or read different parts of a text, then exchange information with others in order to complete a task.

> Ex   Learners in three groups hear different versions of an encounter with aliens. Together with other learners, they complete comprehension questions based on all three descriptions of the encounter.

In the classroom, **Jigsaw tasks** are an excellent way to integrate the skills, as learners read or listen to a text, and speak and listen to others to reconstruct the information in the text. Most written texts can be made into a jigsaw activity easily. Managing a jigsaw listening exercise is more challenging as it requires multiple tape recorders, enough space to listen without disturbing other groups, and time.

Further Reading |||||||||||||||||||||||||||||||||||||||||||||||||||||||||||||||||||||||||

Positive Evidence vs. Negative Evidence

1. Positive Evidence

학습자에게 제공되는 목표 언어의 정확하고 올바른 입력(well-formed sentences to which learners are exposed)

① The most obviously necessary requirement for learning

② It can be authentic or modified. If modified, it can be simplified or elaborated.

③ 학습자들은 이와 같은 언어적 입력을 구어(spoken language), 문어(written language), 제스처와 같은 시각적 언어(visual language in the case of sign language) 등을 통해 받을 수 있다.

2. Negative Evidence

학습자의 발화의 부정확성에 대해 언급하는 정보 유형(information that is provided to learners concerning the incorrectness of an utterance)

① **Pre-emptive**: occurring before an actual error – as in a classroom context. 오류가 실제로 발생하기 이전에 제공되는 오류에 대한 정보를 가리킨다.

② **Reactive**: 실제 일어난 오류에 대한 교정적 정보로서, 명시적인 형태와 묵시적인 형태가 있다.

> ▶ **Explicit Correction**
>
> The teacher directly tells a student what the mistake was and provides the correct answer. For example, she might say, "oh, you mean...," or "you should say...," or "the correct form of this verb form is...". An alternative of this strategy is to ask a peer student, other than the one who committed the error, to provide the correct answer.
>
> T: Where did you go after class yesterday?
> S: I go home.
> T: 'Go' is not the correct past tense form. You need to say, "I went home."

▶ **Recast**

Recasts are complex discourse structures that have been said to contain positive evidence (a model of the correct form), and negative feedback (since the correct form is juxtaposed with the non-target like form) in an environment where the positive evidence is enhanced (because of juxtaposition). If learners do not selectively attend to and recognize the negative feedback contained in recasts, then the documented contribution of recasts to learning might be attributed to the positive evidence they contain, or to the enhanced salience of the positive evidence.

T: What did you do yesterday?
S: I go shopping.
T: Oh, *you went shopping*. Where did you go?
S: I went to IFC mall.

Further Reading

Pushed Output, Uptake, Modified Output

According to Merrill Swain, there are three specific functions of output; they are as follows:

1. The Noticing/Triggering Function

It refers to the awareness or "noticing" students find when they cannot say or write exactly what they need for conveying meaning. With the use of this function, learners realize there are some linguistics problems they need to manage, so that, it pushes the student to look for the adequate knowledge they require for completing the new discovered gap.

"Learners may notice that they cannot say what they want to say in the target language." (Swain, 1995) Noticing this "hole" (Doughty and Williams, 1998) may be an important step to noticing the gap.

2. The Hypothesis—Testing Function

This function suggests learners may use the method of "trial and error" for testing her/his production expecting to receive a feedback. This feedback can be applied in two ways: recasts and elicitations or clarifications requests.

3. The Metalinguistic(reflective function) Function

Language is seen as a tool conducive to reflection on the language used by the teacher, their partners and the student himself/herself. (Vigotsky's sociocultural theory)

When explaining this theory, it is necessary to highlight the importance of the negotiation of meaning, which is not simply related to understand the meaning of the message the transmitter sends to the receiver despite the problems in its structure, but **a clear, precisely, coherently and appropriately message = Pushed output.**

> ▶ The term **uptake** is used to refer "to a learner's utterance that immediately follows the teacher's feedback and that constitutes a reaction in some way to the teacher's intention to draw attention to some aspect of the students initial utterance."

Chapter
03

언어 분석 및 중간언어

언어 분석 및 중간언어

01 \ 대조 분석 가설 – Contrastive Analysis Hypothesis

1 개념

(1) 행동주의와 구조주의를 기반으로 한 **대조 분석**은 제2언어 습득을 방해하는 요인을 모국어의 간섭(**interference**)으로 보고 모국어와 L2의 차이점을 파악해 제2언어 학습에서의 어려움을 덜고자 했다.

Contrastive Analysis Hypothesis is an approach to the study of SLA which involves predicting and explaining learner problems based on a comparison of L1 and L2 to determine similarities and differences. The CAH claimed that the principal barrier to second language acquisition is the **interference** of the first language system with the second language system. The goal of CAH is to isolate what needs to be learned and what does not need to be learned in a second language learning situation.

(2) **단계**

description → selection → contrast → prediction

2 분류

(1) Strong Version

오류가 발생하기 전 두 언어의 차이점을 기술해 학습의 어려움을 예측하고 오류의 출현을 막고자 한다.

One could predict the patterns that will cause difficulty in learning, and those that will not cause difficulty, by comparing systematically the language to be learned with the native language.

(2) Weak Version

실제 언어 학습 후 발생하는 학습자의 오류를 토대로 두 언어를 대조 분석해 오류의 근원을 밝히고자 한다.

Unlike the strong version, it begins with the comparison after the actual problem occurred. That is, based on the actual and recurring difficulties exhibited in the learner's performance, it attempts to account for the differences between the native language and the target language.

3) 대조 분석의 한계점

언어 학습 과정에서 발생하는 오류의 근원을 모국어로만 한정했다. 즉, 학습자의 오류가 모국어의 간섭 이외의 것에서 발생할 수 있는 점을 간과했다.

The most of the errors learners make in L2 cannot be traced to the differences between L1 and L2. In addition, regardless of the features of the students' first languages, they appear to go through similar variable stages in the second language. As a result of the finding that main aspects of learners' language could not be explained by the CAH, a number of researchers began to take a different approach to analysing learners' errors. This approach, which was developed during the 1970s, became known as **'error analysis'** and involved detailed description and analysis of the kinds or errors second language learners make.

Plus ➕

Positive Transfer vs. Negative Transfer

Transfer means the transfer of elements acquired in L1 to the target L2.

1. **Positive (facilitating) Transfer**
   When the same structure is appropriate in both languages.

2. **Negative (interference) Transfer**
   When the L1 structure is used inappropriately in the L2.

4 Cross Linguistic Influence

Cross-linguistic influence(CLI) is typically defined as the influence that knowledge of one language has on an individual's learning or use of another language. This influence can involve various aspects of language. For example, for a native speaker of Spanish who is learning English, CLI may lead to Spanish-sounding pronunciation when speaking English (e.g., pronouncing "zoo" like "soo"), Spanish word or sentence order when writing in English (e.g., writing "The car red is mine," instead of "The red car is mine"), or comprehension of Spanish words that look or sound similar to English words (e.g., "turista" = "tourist").

In the Classroom

Contrastive analysis is based on behaviorism. It considers L1 to be mainly in interference to the mastery of L2. In order to become proficient in L2, the habits of L1 need to be "broken" before the habits of L2 can become firmly established. Thus, audiolingualism, its most well-known manifestation, presented us with mim-mem drills and practice with minimal pairs such as *chew* and *shoe* (for Spanish speakers), *glass* and *grass* (for Korean speakers), and dialogues to be memorized so that students could avoid errors in the new language and take on its proper forms.

Students who learn English as a foreign language already have a deep knowledge of at least one other language, and where L1 and English come into contact with each other there are often confusions which provoke errors in a learner's use of English. This can be at the **level of sounds**: Korean, for example, does not have a phonemic distinction between /r/ and /l/ and Korean speakers may well say *lice* when they mean *rice*. It can be at **the level of grammar** where a student's first language has a subtly different system: our students often have trouble with *article usage* and the *present perfect* because Korean doesn't have such a form. Thus, in order to solve the problems, the teacher should provide students with meaningful minimal pairs practice at the level of sounds and grammar.

02 \ 학습자 언어와 오류 분석 – Learner Language and Error Analysis

1 학습자 언어 – Interlanguage

(1) 개념

중간언어(interlanguage)란 학습자가 목표어를 습득하는 과정 중 발생하는 것으로, 모국어와 목표어의 중간에 있는 불완전한 언어 체계를 말한다.

Interlanguage means an intermediate system located somewhere between the learner's native language and the target language, but governed by its own unique and coherent internalized rule system that rarely becomes totally congruent with the system of the second language.

(2) 중간언어의 특징

① **Learner language is systematic**: 중간언어는 나름의 일정한 체계를 가진다. 그러나 모든 학습자가 똑같은 중간언어 체계를 갖는 것은 아니다.

At any particular stage of development, the IL is governed by rules which constitute the learner's internal grammar.

> Ex 부정문에 관한 규칙에 대해서 문두에 No나 Not을 사용하는 경우
> No speak English. (= I don't speak English.)
> No come. (= I'm not coming.)

② **Learner language is variable**: 중간언어의 불완전한 특성으로 인한 것으로, 변이성이란 어떤 의미를 나타내기 위해 맥락에 따라 중간언어가 다른 형태로 나타나는 특징을 말한다.

Although the IL is systematic, differences in context result in different patterns of language use.

> Ex I don't know anything.
> I don't know nothing.

③ **Learner language is dynamic**: 중간언어의 규칙 체계는 <u>끊임없이 수정되고 자체적으로도 변화·발전</u>한다.

The learners' system changes frequently, resulting in a succession of interim grammars. This change is not a steady progression, but discontinuous progression from stable to stable plateau.

(3) 중간언어의 발달 단계

presystematic ⟶ emergent ⟶ systematic ⟶ stabilization

① 체계 전 단계(presystematic stage): <u>무작위 오류(random errors)</u>가 나타나는 단계로, 목표어 체계를 파악하지 못하고 실수를 많이 하는 시기이다.

The first is a stage of random errors, a stage called "presystematic," in which the learner is only vaguely aware that there is some systematic order to a particular class of items.

> **Ex** John *cans* sing. I *can to sing.*

② 출현 단계(emergent stage): The second, or emergent, stage of learner language finds the <u>learner growing in consistency in linguistic production.</u> The learner has begun to discern a system and to internalize certain rules. In general the learner is still, <u>at this stage, unable to correct error when they are pointed out by someone else.</u>

ⓐ 학습자는 발화를 일관성 있게 발전시켜 내재화하기 시작한다.
ⓑ 중간언어에 대한 자신감이 나타나서 교사의 조언을 거부하기도 한다.
ⓒ Backsliding 현상이 지배적이다.
ⓓ 구문과 화제의 회피가 전형적으로 일어난다.
ⓔ 오류 지적 시 수정을 하지 못한다.

Plus ➕

Backsliding

The emergent stage is characterized by some "backsliding" in which the learner seems to have grasped a rule or principle and then regresses to some previous stage.

외국어 학습자가 목표어의 규칙을 습득하는 방향으로 나가는 것이 아니라 더 안정되고 용이하다고 생각되는 중간언어 형태에 의존해 의사 전달을 시도하는 현상을 말한다. 이는 학습자가 목표어 규칙을 지니고 있으면서 어떤 감정적 불안이나 상황적 요인 때문에 정확한 규칙을 이용할 수 없는 경우에 출현한다.

Example ❶

학습자의 발화를 통해 학습자의 중간언어 발달 단계 및 그 근거를 기술하시오.

Student : I go New York.
Teacher : You're going to New York?
Student : (*doesn't understand*) What?
Teacher : You will go to New York.
Student : Yes.
Teacher : When?
Student : 1972.
Teacher : Oh, you went to New York in 1972.
Student : Yes, I go New York 1972.

③ 체계적 단계(systematic stage): A third stage is a truly systematic stage in which the learner is now able to manifest more consistency in producing the second language. While those rules that are stored in the learner's brain are still not all well-formed, they are more internally self-consistent and, of course, they more closely approximate the target language system.

ⓐ 일관성 있게 규칙을 내재화한다.
ⓑ 오류가 제시될 때 그것을 수정할 수 있다.

Example ❷

학습자의 발화를 통해 학습자의 중간언어 발달 단계 및 그 근거를 기술하시오.

Student : Many fish are in the lake. These fish *are serving* in the restaurants near the lake.
Teacher : (*laughing*) The fish *are serving*?
Student : (*laughing*) Oh, no, the fish *are served* in the restaurants!

④ 안정화 단계(stabilization stage, postsystematic stage): At the final stage called the stabilization stage, the learner has relatively few errors and has mastered the system to the point that fluency and intended meanings are not problematic. This fourth stage is characterized by the learner's ability to self-correct. At this point learners can stabilize too fast, allowing minor errors to slip by undetected, and thus manifest **fossilization** of their language.

ⓐ 목표어를 유창하게 구사할 수 있다.
ⓑ 오류를 범하지 않으며, 범하더라도 스스로 수정(self-correction)할 능력이 있다.
ⓒ 화석화 현상(fossilization)이 발생한다.

Plus ➕

Fossilization(화석화 현상)
목표어를 유창하게 사용하는 학습자가 특정 표현을 지속적으로 부정확하게 사용하는 경우를 일컫는다. 화석화 현상을 막기 위해 교사는 학습자가 지속적으로 오류를 범하는 표현에 대해 적절한 피드백을 사용해 자체적으로 수정하도록 해야 한다.
Fossilization refers to the process in which incorrect language becomes a habit and cannot easily be corrected.

1. **In the classroom**
   Errors in general take time to correct but a fossilized error may never be corrected unless the learner sees a reason to do so, e.g. if it is seriously hindering communication. Teachers can help learners notice their fossilized errors by for example recording them speaking, or by asking them to keep a record of written errors as part of a language portfolio.

2. **Causes of Fossilization**
   ① lack of negative feedback on error in the form of self-monitoring
   ② insensitivity to negative feedback
   ③ provision of positive feedback on successful communication despite error
   ④ lack of access to various components of UG

Plus ⊕

U-shaped Learning

U-shaped patterns reflect three stages of linguistic use.

Stage 1: A learner produces some linguistic form that conforms to target-like norms (error-free).

Stage 2: A learner appears to lose what he or she knew at Stage 1, deviating from the target language norms (overgeneralization & backsliding).

Stage 3: This stage looks just like Stage 1 in that there is again correct target language usage.

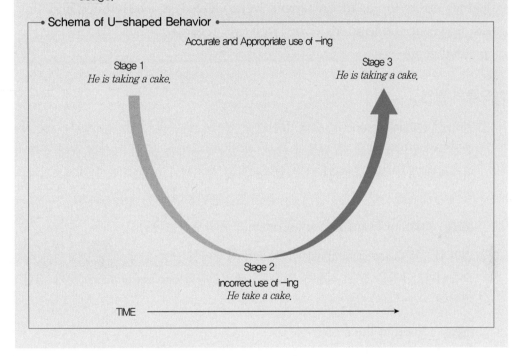

• Schema of U-shaped Behavior •

Accurate and Appropriate use of -ing

Stage 1
He is taking a cake.

Stage 3
He is taking a cake.

Stage 2
incorrect use of -ing
He take a cake.

TIME

(4) 시사점

외국어 학습은 체계적인 발달 과정으로, 교실에서의 수업은 학습자들의 중간언어 발달 단계의 속도와 외국어 학습의 성공도에 영향을 준다. 그러므로 교사는 학습자들이 중간언어의 단계들을 거쳐 점차 목표어에 도달하게 되는 것을 이해하고 오류를 하나의 학습 과정으로 규정해 더 나은 중간언어 단계로 도달할 수 있도록 도와야 한다. 따라서 교사는 학습자가 보다 나은 중간언어 단계에 이르도록 학습자의 부정확한 언어 형태에 대해 적절한 피드백(feedback)을 제공해 스스로 오류를 수정(self-correction)할 수 있도록 해야 한다.

2 오류 분석

(1) 개념

학습자의 오류의 원인을 모국어로 한정시키고 오류를 잘못된 학습의 결과로 여겨 오류를 방지하고자 했던 대조 분석과는 달리, 오류 분석은 학습자의 오류를 목표어의 체계에 도달하는 하나의 과정(중간언어, interlanguage)이라 인식하고 학습자의 오류를 관찰·분석·시정하고자 한다.

Error Analysis is the approach based on the description and analysis of actual learner errors in L2. In CA, errors were viewed as interference and sins. In EA, however, the learner's errors were not regarded as sins that needed to be avoided at all.

(2) 오류의 원인

① 언어 간 전이(interference): 모국어의 간섭 현상으로 인해 출현하는 오류를 일컫는다. 한국인이 영어를 배울 때 발음과 관사·전치사의 올바른 사용, 통사적 규칙 등에 있어 어려움을 겪는 것은 영어와 다른 한국어라는 선지식이 내재돼 간섭을 일으키기 때문이다.

> Ex 'take an exam'을 'see an exam'으로 표현하는 경우

② 언어 내 전이(intralingual transfer): 목표어 자체에서 오는 간섭 현상으로 인해 출현한 오류이다. 규칙을 잘못 적용한 경우로, 과잉일반화(overgeneralization)가 전형적인 예이다.

> Ex I goed to the store.

③ 학습 환경(context of learning): 교재나 교사의 오류로 인해 학습자의 잘못된 수행이 일어난 경우이다.

> Ex 교실 학습에서 'point to'와 'point out'의 차이에 대한 혼란스러운 교수가 이뤄질 경우 실제 언어 사용 시 오류가 발생할 수 있다.

④ 의사소통 전략(communication strategies): 자신의 언어적 한계를 극복하기 위해 사용하는 전략적 방법으로, 의사소통 전략에 의해 오류가 발생할 수 있다.

> Ex 'vegetarian'을 'vegetarianist'로 나타내는 것처럼 조어를 만들어 사용하는 경우 (word coinage)

(3) 오류의 기술 및 범주

① 표면적 특성에 따른 범주(Dulay, Burt & Krashen, 1982)

    ⓐ **Addition**: 정상적인 발화에 출현해서는 안 되는 부분이 출현한 경우

        Ex He can *do* sing very well.

    ⓑ **Omission**: 정상적인 발화에 출현해야 할 부분이 생략된 경우

        Ex She - sleeping.

    ⓒ **Substitution**: 정상적인 발화에 출현해야 할 부분이 다른 것으로 대체돼 나타난 경우

        Ex She *gaved* it to him.

    ⓓ **Misordering**: 정상적인 발화의 어순을 갖추지 못한 경우

        Ex I *to the store* went.

② 의사소통의 흐름에 따른 범주(Burt & Kiparsky, 1972)

    ⓐ **Global error**: 통사 구조 및 담화상에서 빚어지는 오류로서 메시지가 잘 전달되지 않는다. 따라서 의사소통의 단절을 가져오므로 반드시 수정돼야 한다.

    ⓑ **Local error**: 문장 일부분만 잘못된 경우로서 화자가 의도한 메시지 전달이 가능하다. 따라서 반드시 수정될 필요는 없다.

(4) 오류의 역할 및 수정 범위

① 오류(error)란 학습자가 여러 가지 변인으로 인해 잘못된 목표어(incorrect form/non-target-like form)를 사용하는 것으로, 적절한 feedback이 학습자의 중간언어 체계를 한 단계 높일 수 있다. 따라서 이때 교사의 오류의 평가가 학습자의 언어적 발달에 중요한 영향을 미칠 수 있다.

② 오류 수정의 기준은 학습 목표에 따라 달라질 수 있으며, <u>학습 목표가 언어의 유창성에 있다면 의사소통의 단절로서 global error가 local error보다 더 심각한 것으로 평가되기 때문에 반드시 global error를 수정해야 한다.</u> 또한, <u>학습 목표가 정확성에 초점을 둘 경우 표면적인 오류도 수정</u>해야 한다.

③ 오류 수정 시에는 학습자의 언어적 수준과 정서적인 측면을 고려하는 것이 바람직하다. 반면에 학습 목표가 정확성에 있다면 학습자의 <u>반복되는 local error도 화석화 현상 (fossilization)을 막기 위해 수정</u>돼야 한다.

(5) 교실에서의 Feedback

교사의 feedback은 학습자의 제2언어 학습에 대한 효과와 성공에 영향을 준다. 특히 학습자의 부정확한 언어 사용에 대한 부정적인 피드백은 학습자로 하여금 자신의 발화를 돌아보게 하고 보다 정확한 발화를 사용하도록 유도함으로써 제2언어 습득을 가속화할 수 있다. 아울러 학습자의 정확한 언어 사용을 위해 전통적인 방식의 명시적 수정보다는 의사소통 내에서 자연스러운 언어 사용에 대한 격려로 묵시적인 피드백을 장려하고 있다. 하지만, 어떤 피드백을 사용할 것인가는 교실 수업의 목적과 학습자의 proficiency level 및 context에 따라 적절하게 선택돼야 한다.

Corrective feedback can be accomplished in different ways. Explicit correction of an error and explanation of a language rule helps clarify what is wrong with a response so that a student can be aware of how to produce the correct form in the future.

Negative feedback may be explicit or implicit, and it seems that most traditional studies have focused on the former, directing participants' attention to forms, whereas, more recent studies have been investigating the effectiveness of implicit negative feedback, such as recasts. Recasting is defined as the corrective reformulation of an erroneous utterance. It occurs in the course of a natural interaction during which the focus is on form as opposed to forms.

Another version of corrective feedback is requesting clarification of an answer. A teacher can ask for the student to state it again or ask the student to explain what was meant in their response. Metalinguistic clues can also help a teacher elicit the correct response from a student. By giving students clues about the correct format of the language, students may figure it out on their own and produce the proper utterance. Finally, repetition also is an easy corrective feedback technique. Teachers can repeat the incorrect answer given by a student in a different tone, so that the student knows that it is incorrect. This will signal the student to try again and fix the mistake.

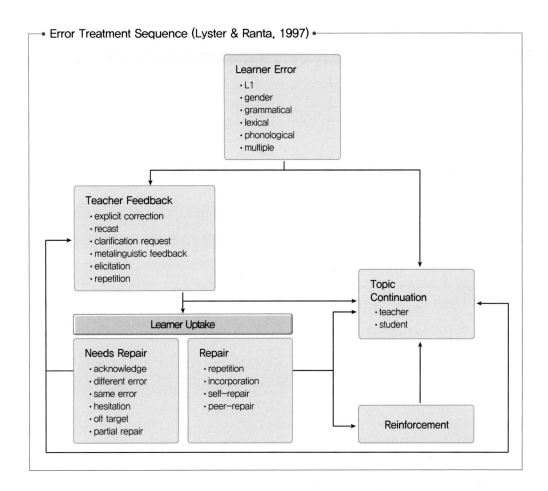

- Error Treatment Sequence (Lyster & Ranta, 1997)

① **Explicit correction**: A teacher provides the correct form, he or she clearly indicates that what the student had said was incorrect, for example, "Oh, you mean...," "You should say..."

> **Ex** L : When I have twelve years old...
>
> T : No, not *have*. You mean, "When I *was* twelve years old..."

② **Recasts**: A teacher reformulates all or part of a student's utterance, minus the error. Recasts are generally implicit.

> **Ex** L : He *come* into the room.
>
> T : Yes, he *came* into the room, What happened next?

③ **Clarification requests**: A teacher indicates to students either that their utterance has been misunderstood or that the utterance is ill-formed in some way and that a repetition or a reformulation is required. A clarification request includes phrases such as "Pardon me.," "What do you mean by...?" and so on.

> Ex : L : We go to July 4 fireworks and crackers were very loud.
> T : Pardon me?

④ **Metalinguistic feedback**: It contains comments, information, or questions related to the well-formedness of the student's utterance, without explicitly providing the correct form.

> Ex : L : I am here since January.
> T : Well, okay, but remember we talked about the present perfect tense last week?

⑤ **Elicitation**: Teachers use to directly elicit the correct form from the student using questions ("How do we say X in French?"), incomplete sentences ("It's a...") and asking students to reformulate their utterance.

> Ex : L : (*to another student*) What means this word?
> T : Uh, Luis, how do we say that in English? What does...?
> L : Ah, what does the word mean?

⑥ **Repetition**: A teacher repeats the student's erroneous utterance. In most cases, teachers adjust their intonation so as to highlight the error.

> Ex : L : When I have twelve years old...
> T : Have?

Read the classroom talk below and follow the directions.

T : What did you do last Sunday?
S : Movie.
T : Excuse me?
S : I see a movie.
T : You saw a movie?
S : Yes, I see a movie.
T : But you saw a movie LAST Sunday, and last Sunday is in the past, right?
S : Oh, yes, Right.
T : The correct verb is SAW, not SEE.

Identify each utterance of the given feedback type from the dialogue above.

Feedback Type	Example
Explicit Correction	①
Recast	②
Clarification Requests	③
Metalinguistic Feedback	④

➡ ① The correct verb is SAW, not SEE.
② You saw a movie?
③ Excuse me?
④ But you saw a movie LAST Sunday, and last Sunday is in the past, right?

03 \ 담화 분석

1 개념

담화란 글의 흐름 및 연속체를 뜻하는데, 담화 분석은 문장 간의 관계를 통해 글의 결합력과 통일성을 연구하는 것이다. 또한 담화 분석은 담화에서 사용된 언어 형식과 기능 간의 관계를 통해 언어가 사용되는 상황과 언어를 분석한다.

Discourse analysis serves as a device for systematically describing the kinds of interactions that occur in language classrooms. Discourse analysts give attention not only to the function of individual utterances but also to how these utterances combine to form larger discoursal units.

2 담화의 구성 요건

> ▶ **Cohesion** refers to connectivity in a text.
> ▶ **Coherence** refers to how easy it is to understand the writing.

(1) Cohesion(결합력)

결합력은 글의 요소들이 연관돼 있는 정도로 주로 단어의 반복과 상위 단어, 인칭대명사·지시대명사의 사용 등에 의해 결정된다. 또한 결합력은 일관성을 보완하는 요소이지만 결합력이 있다고 해서 반드시 일관성 있는 텍스트라고 할 수는 없다.

If a text is cohesive, its elements are connected. Cohesion is the use of grammatical and lexical means to achieve connected text, either spoken or written. Unlike coherence, which different readers or listeners may experience to varying degrees, cohesion is a stable property of text. And while cohesion may help make a text coherent, it cannot guarantee it.

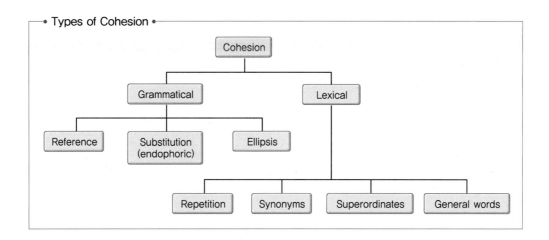

• Types of Cohesion •

- Cohesion
  - Grammatical
    - Reference
    - Substitution (endophoric)
    - Ellipsis
  - Lexical
    - Repetition
    - Synonyms
    - Superordinates
    - General words

(2) Coherence(일관성)

일관성은 텍스트를 구성하는 중요한 요소 중의 하나로, 텍스트 속 문장들이 서로 연관돼 논리적 일관성을 유지하는지의 문제이다. 따라서 결합 장치(cohesive device)가 없어도 하나의 주제(topic) 안에서 문장들이 논리적 관계를 이루고 있다면 일관성 있는 텍스트 (coherent text)가 될 수 있다.

If a text is coherent, it makes sense. The coherent sentences are related to each other, and relate in our background knowledge of the world.

① The following paragraph is both coherent and cohesive:

> Ex ┊ "My favourite colour is blue. I like it because it is calming and it relaxes me. I often go outside in the summer and lie on the grass and look into the clear sky when I am stressed. For this reason, I'd have to say my favourite colour is blue."

② Cohesion with NO Coherence

> Ex ┊ "My favourite colour is blue. Blue sports cars go very fast. Driving in this way is dangerous and can cause many car crashes. I had a car accident once and broke my leg. I was very sad because I had to miss a holiday in Europe because of the injury."

As you can see, there is plenty of cohesion here. The sentences connect clearly together but if you read the paragraph, it really makes no sense— I start talking about blue and I finish talking about a holiday in Europe. There is no coherence in this paragraph.

③ Coherence with NO Cohesion

> Ex "We want you to be delighted with this facility. If there is a fault with the toilet please call extn 1071 on the nearest white courtesy phone."

The language and organization of the text are appropriate, especially when we know that the text was written to be read in an airport restroom. Moreover, the two sentences of the text have a logical relation.

3 대화 분석

대화 분석(Conversation Analysis)은 대표적인 담화 분석으로, 말하기 수업에서 대화를 직접 분석하면서 대화상에 갖춰야 하는 격률 등을 학생들에게 지도한다.

(1) 주의 끌기(Attention Getting)

대화를 시작하기 위해서는 우선적으로 주의를 끌어야 하는데, 주의 끌기의 방법으로는 언어적 또는 비언어적인 방법이 있다. 언어적인 방법으로는 "Excuse me", "Sorry", "Sir…" 등의 말을 사용하는 방법이 있고, 비언어적인 방법으로는 눈을 마주치거나 눈에 띄는 행동을 함으로써 주목을 끄는 방법이 있다.

(2) Topic Nomination

주의 끌기에 성공했을 경우, 대화를 이끌어 나가기 위한 주제를 정해야 한다. 대화 주제 정하기는 대화를 이끌고 있는 사람과 상황에 따라 결정해야 한다.

(3) Topic Development

대화의 주제를 정하고 난 뒤, 원만한 대화 전개를 위해 적절하게 대화를 받아주는 turn taking, 대화 중 정확한 이해를 위한 topic clarification, 적절한 순간에 다른 화제로 옮기는 topic shifting, 무례하지 않은 상황에서 화제를 회피하는 topic avoidance 등에 주의를 기울인다.

⑷ Topic Termination

화제 종결은 언어적 또는 비언어적인 방식으로 가능하다. 시계를 쳐다본다거나 상호작용적 언어 기능을 통해 종료할 수 있다.

▶ **Adjacency Pairs**

One of the most common structures to be defined through conversation analysis is the adjacency pair, which is a call and response type of sequential utterances spoken by two different people.

Ex *Offer/Refusal*

Sales clerk : Do you need someone to carry your packages out?
Customer : No thanks. I've got it.

▶ **Conversational Gambits**

Gambits as the conversational signal used to organize utterance and interaction are often employed in classroom discussion: *"In my point of view..."* to express opinion or *"Sorry for interrupting..."* to interrupt someone's speaking.

In the Classroom

Classroom Talk

1. Question Types

① Display Questions: They seek answers in which the information is already known by the teacher. This type of elicitation has been criticised for its lack of authenticity since it is not commonly used in conversation outside the classroom. Extensive use of display questions could be a waste of time. However, it is said that display questions can potentially be central resources which language teachers and students use to organize language lessons and produce language pedagogy. Accordingly, they are an important tool in the classroom, not only for the teacher to be able to check and test their learners, but also as a source of listening practice. One of the first things a beginner learns in English is how to understand and answer display questions.

> Ex   The teacher asks a learner "What is the past simple form of leave?"

② Referential Questions: They require answers which contain information unknown by the teacher, and they are frequently used to call for evaluation or judgment. They are commonly used in regular conversation outside the classroom, hence are believed to encourage students' higher-order thinking skills and authentic use of the second language in the classroom. Many teachers agree that teachers' use of referential questions could prompt students to provide significantly longer and syntactically more complex responses than the use of display questions.

> Ex❶   What do you think about this topic?
> What do you think about animal rights?

> Ex❷   T: Last week we were reading "Kee Knock Stan" (title of a story). What is "Kee Knock Stan," Hyunsoo?
> S: I cannot understand.
> T: Yes. What do you think the postman at the post office would do?
> S: I think I would divide it if the letters are to Hong Kong or other places.
> T: Yes, I think that's a sensible way, right? Good.

Both questions asked by the teacher are "what" questions, but the first one is a "display" question which has only one correct answer, hence "closed." The second is a "referential" question with no pre-determined answer, hence "open."

2. Effective Questioning

효과적인 질문 기법은 학습자가 교사의 질문에 대답할 수 있도록 유도하는 것으로, 질문에 대한 대답을 이끌어 내지 못할 경우 교사는 즉각 자신의 질문을 학습자의 수준에 맞춰 수정해야 할 것이다.

Language teachers in questioning are usually to get their students to engage with the language material actively through speech; so an effective questioning technique is one that elicits fairly prompt, motivated, relevant and full responses. If, on the other hand, their questions result in long silences, or are answered by only the strongest students, or obviously bore the class, or consistently elicit only very brief or unsuccessful answers, then there is probably something wrong.

Thus, when teachers fail to elicit any response from the learners, they often need to modify their questions. There are a number of modification devices used by teachers, including syntactic modifications (such as making the topic salient and decomposing complex structures) and semantic modifications such as paraphrasing difficult words and disambiguation.

For example, in a language classroom, the teacher reads out a sentence describing a dog. She said "So that's a very good descriptive sentence. It tells you exactly what the dog looks like. Can you picture the dog?" The teacher realized that the use of the word "picture" might be a bit beyond the pupils's ability level. Therefore, she modified the question to "If I were to ask you to draw the dog, would you be able to draw the dog?" As a result of her *lexical modification*, the students immediately responded in chorus by saying "yes, yes."

3. Classroom Discourse

① IRE: 대부분의 교실 담화의 구조로 다음과 같다.

> • The teacher *initiates* an assertion or asks a question.
> • The student *responds*.
> • The teacher *evaluates*, by giving an evaluative statement such as "very good" or by asking the same or similar question of another student.

IRE는 학습자들의 어휘력이나 문법적 능력의 내재화 정도를 알아보기 위해 진행되는 교실 담화 구조로, 교사가 assessing questions(한 가지 정확한 답변 및 예측 가능한 답변을 요구하는 질문)를 제시하고 학습자의 답변에 대한 평가를 'very good', 'right', 'excellent' 등으로 제공한다. 그러나 이러한 IRE의 담화는 교실 밖의 의사소통 구조를 담고 있지 않으며, 또한 의미 위주의 담화 형태로 발전해 나가지 않는다.

② IRF: 학습자의 발화에 대한 평가가 아니라, 의미 위주의 담화를 확장시켜 나가는 것에 초점을 두는 담화 구조이다. 대부분의 교실 수업의 상호작용은 Initiation-Response-Feedback(IRF), 즉 교사가 질문하고 학생들이 대답한 뒤 학생들의 대답에 대한 피드백의 형태를 띤다.

> • The teacher *initiates* an assertion or asks a question.
> • The students *responds*.
> • The teacher *provides feedback* in order to encourage students to think and to perform at higher levels (e.g. "Tell me more! Are you saying that...?)

본 담화 형태에서 교사는 assisting questions를 통해 학습자가 내용과 주제에 초점을 둬 생각하고 자신의 생각을 보다 정교하게 말할 수 있도록 유도한다. 가령, 교사는 "What do you mean by that?" / "That's incredible" / "Could you explain that a little more?" 등의 assisting question을 제시할 수 있다. 누가 말을 하고 언제 해야 할 것인지를 교사에 의해 통제받는 IRE의 담화 구조에서, 지배적인 교실 수업을 받고 있는 학습자들은 자연스럽게 대화에 참여하며 자연스러운 turn-taking을 할 수 있는 기회를 제공받아야 한다.

Chapter
04

학습자 변인

학습자 변인

Learner characteristics include a learner's motivation, learning styles, learning strategies and past language learning experience. They are factors which influence learners' attitude to learning a language, how they learn it, how they respond to different teaching styles and approaches in the classroom, and how successful they are at learning a language.

01 \ 인지적 요인(Cognitive Domain)

인지적 요인에는 개인에 따라 방식이 달라지는 학습 양식(learning style)과 특정 상황에서 특정 과제를 해결하기 위해 개인이 선택하는 전략(learner strategy)이 있다.

1 Learning Style

여기에 제시된 모든 학습 양식은 과제의 유형에 따라 성공적인 학습을 위해 모두 필요하므로, 교사는 학습자의 선호 유형과 부족한 학습 양식을 파악하고 과제를 통해 상호 보완적인 수업(strategies-based instruction)을 진행해야 한다.

Learning styles are the ways in which a leaner naturally prefers to take in, process and remember information and skills. Our learning style influences how we like to learn and how we learn best.

(1) 장독립형(Field Independence) vs. 장의존형(Field Dependence)

① 장독립형 학습자: 전체의 장(field)에 산재해 있는 개별적 항목 및 세부 사항에 주목하므로 설명과 반복 훈련, 연습 등의 교실 수업에 더 적합하다.

In the field-dependent/independent model of cognitive or learning style, a field-independent learning style is defined by a tendency to separate details from the surrounding context. It can be compared to a field-dependent learning style, which is defined by a relative inability to distinguish detail from other information around it. Theorists define these two cognitive styles in terms of how they are psychologically different—which makes this a useful model for teachers trying to understand their learners.

② 장의존형 학습자: 전체 맥락을 통해서 일반화하며 감정이입(empathy)이 잘 되고 사교적인 스타일로, 의사소통 측면의 학습과 협동 학습에 유리하다.

Field dependent learners prefer to work with others to achieve a common goal. They are greatly influenced by the teacher and very often interact with the him/her. They are more sensitive to others' feelings, opinions, and ideas. They like to practice and learn by experimentation (as opposed to conceptual discussion) before starting the task ("global learners").

04

Further Reading

FI vs. FD

In cognitive style, the field dependent learners are those learners who are most affected by their environment. They are inclined to overall field learning and tend to get the whole idea whereas the field independent learners conduct an analytical procedure and are more likely to break a model into different sections and details and tend to depend on their inner knowledge and analyze problems all by themselves without reference to the frame or the environment.

Considering field dependent-independent cognitive styles effects on teaching and learning, and especially on the students' course selection, studies show that field independent student had better academic achievement than field dependent students. The research also showed that if the educational subjects and materials conform to students' cognitive styles, it will lead to a better achievement. Also, the studies revealed that if the field dependents and field independents are placed in homogeneous groups compared with being in the heterogeneous groups, they would show a better improvement.

Field Independence	Field Dependence
• like to analyze information into its component parts and distinguish the essential from the inessential. • prefer to find solutions to problems for themselves. • are more particularistic and analytic.	• like to deal with information structures as wholes. • are sociable and work well in groups. • have difficulty discerning a figure apart from the field. • are more global and holistic in processing new information.

(2) 좌뇌(Left Brain) vs. 우뇌(Right Brain)

The theory is that people are either **left-brained** or **right-brained**, meaning that one side of their brain is dominant. If you're mostly analytical and methodical in your thinking, you're said to be left-brained. If you tend to be more creative or artistic, you're thought to be right-brained.

① 좌뇌: 논리적·분석적 사고 및 수사학적·선형적 정보처리에 능한 학습 유형으로, 장독립형 학습 환경에 적합하다.

The left brain is more verbal, analytical, and orderly than the right brain. It's sometimes called the digital brain. It's better at things like *reading*, *writing*, and *computations*. The left brain is also connected to: logic, sequencing, linear thinking, mathematics, facts, thinking in words

② 우뇌: 시각·촉각·청각적 이미지로 지각 및 기억해 통합적·전체적·정서적 정보 처리에 효과적인 학습 유형으로, 장의존형 학습 환경에 적합하다.

The right brain is more visual and intuitive. It's sometimes referred to as the analog brain. It has a more creative and less organized way of thinking. The right brain is also connected to: imagination, holistic thinking, intuition, arts, rhythm, nonverbal cues, feelings visualization

③ 시사점: 좌뇌와 우뇌는 그 기능을 달리하지만, 언어 학습에는 두 기능이 하나의 팀으로 작용하기 때문에 좌뇌와 우뇌의 균형을 맞추는 전략적인 수업이 필요하다.

Your left and right brain are members of a team. Use both sides and your brain will stay balanced.

For example, the left brain is credited with language, but the right brain helps you understand context and tone. The left brain handles mathematical equations, but right brain helps out with comparisons and rough estimates.

In the Classroom

Left Brain vs. Right Brain: Tips and Tricks

1. Left Brain

- Spend some time each day reading, writing, or both.
- Never stop learning. Take a class, go to a lecture, or try to acquire a new skill.
- Tackle challenging crossword and sudoku puzzles.
- Play memory games, board games, card games, or video games.
- Take on a new hobby that requires you to focus.

2. Right Brain

- When you get new ideas, write them down and work on developing them further.
- Brainstorm. When faced with a problem, try to find several ways to get to a solution.
- When doing simple chores, such as washing the dishes, leave the TV off and let your mind wander to new places.
- Rest, relax, and laugh to let your creative juices flow.

⑶ **모호함에 대한 관용**(Ambiguity Tolerance)

외국어 학습 시 모국어와 다른 언어 규칙이나 문화에 대해 관용적인 태도를 취해야 더 성공적으로 제2언어를 습득할 수 있다.

It entails <u>an ability to deal with ambiguous new stimuli without frustration</u> and without appeals to authority. Successful language learning necessitates tolerance of such ambiguities, at least for interim periods or stages, during which time ambiguous items are given a chance to become resolved.

(4) 숙고형(Reflectivity) vs. 충동형(Impulsivity)

It is usually stated that reflective learners tend to be slower at approaching a task, but accurate, whereas impulsive learners need less time for an answer but tend to make more mistakes as a result of their rapid guesses.

① 숙고형 학습자: 체계적이고 논리적인 사고에 의해 학습하기 때문에 문제 해결에 다소 시간이 걸리지만 충동형보다 오류를 적게 발생시킨다.

They seem to be overtly focused and their deep concentration levels make quick decisions almost impossible.

② 충동형 학습자: 신속하고 직관적으로 과제를 처리하며, 문맥을 통한 유추가 뛰어나기 때문에 오류가 발생하더라도 유추를 통해 과제를 처리할 수 있다.

Impulsive learners are globalized in their thinking process and they can create a quick mental picture of patterns and objects or even outlines of lessons.

③ How impulsivity and reflectivity can affect language learning? Reflective learners are those who seek accuracy, whereas, impulsive learner prefer to learn more roughly rather than more precisely. The former groups avoid making mistakes, while the latter might be more open to making mistakes.

(5) 시각형(Visual Style) vs. 청각형(Auditory Style)

Visual learners tend to prefer reading, studying chart, drawings, and other graphic information, while auditory learners prefer listening to lectures and audiotapes.

Visual and auditory learning styles are among the most significant perceptual learning styles. It is assumed that language teaching methods that have interactive forms are more suitable for kinesthetic, visual and auditory learners. Such interaction, however, should be based on learners' learning styles. Therefore, role models in audiolingual method can aid visual learners. On the other hand, total physical approach can be suitable for kinesthetic learners and listening activities may suit auditory learners. It should be mentioned that all language teaching methods might have activities that foster visual, auditory or kinesthetic learning.

Plus ➕

1. Four Learning Styles

General Learning Style	Main Characteristics
Concrete Learning Style	direct means of processing information; people orientated; spontaneous; imaginative; emotional; dislikes routinized learning; prefers kinesthetic modality
Analytical Learning Style	focuses on specific problems and proceeds by means of hypothetical-deductive reasoning; object-orientated; independent; dislikes failure; prefers logical, didactic presentation
Communicative Learning Style	fairly independent; highly adaptable and flexible; responsive to facts that do not fit; prefers social learning and a communicative approach; enjoys taking decisions
Authority-orientated Learning Style	reliant on other people; needs teacher's directions and explanations; likes a structured learning environment; intolerant of facts that do not fit; prefers a sequential progression; dislikes discovery learning

2. The Learning Benefits of Learning Styles

Styles	SLA Advantages?
Left-brain Processing	• analyzing linguistic systems, rules, structures, definitions • perceiving the logic of language systems
Right-brain Processing	• integrating diverse linguistic input • comprehending and producing metaphors
Field Independence	• expressing and comprehending key ideas concisely • remembering lexical and syntactic details
Field Dependence	• getting the overall gist of oral and written input • "reading between the lines" of oral and written input
Ambiguity Tolerance	• transcending linguistic complexity perceived as difficult • maintaining attention to a difficult conversation or text
Ambiguity Intolerance	• ascertaining order and system within complexity • questioning/clarifying misunderstood information
Reflectivity	• taking time to mentally sort through linguistic complexity • speaking out only when certain of linguistic systems
Impulsivity	• taking linguistic risks in the face of possible error • taking initiative in conversations

In the Classroom |||||||||||||||||||||||||||||||||||||||||||||||||||||||||||||||||||||||||||||||||||||||||||||||||||||||||||||

Discovering Students' Learning Styles

Read about two different students in the same English class.

S1 : Maria is eighteen years old and wants to go to a university in the United States. She has been an excellent student all her life, getting lots of A's on her report cards. In her English class, she is very shy. She seldom speaks in class unless the teacher calls on her. Whenever she speaks English, she likes to plan what she is going to say, so she takes a long time to speak out any things. Her English has good grammar, but her pronunciation is not very clear. She prefers to write things down in English before saying them. She has high scores on her written quizzes and tests, but her scores on pronunciation quizzes are only average. She studies very hard, by herself, outside class. She almost never goes to parties.

S2 : Manuel is also eighteen years old and also wants to go to a university in the United States. His grades in school have been average. In his English class he talks a lot. He always raises his hand to speak. He never really plans what he is going to say. His grammar is average, but his pronunciation is excellent and he talks very naturally. He doesn't write things down very often. His written test scores are average, but on pronunciation quizzes he usually gets an A+. Outside class, Manuel rarely studies, but he has a lot of American friends and talks with them a lot. He loves to go to parties.

② Learner Strategy

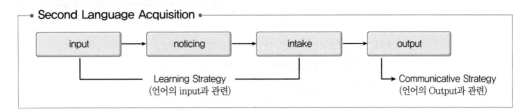

(1) Learning Strategy

Language learning strategies represent specific actions, behaviors, steps, or techniques that students (often intentionally) use to improve their progress in developing L2 skills. These strategies can facilitate the internalization, storage, retrieval, or use of the new language. Strategies are tools for the self-directed involvement necessary for developing communicative ability.

학습에 능한 학습자들(effective language learners)은 전략 사용의 필요성과 이유를 명확히 인지하고 있으며, 특정한 과업에 효과적인 전략을 선별적으로 사용할 수 있다. 반면, 학업에 부진한 학습자들(less effective learners)도 전략 사용에 대한 의식을 갖고는 있으나, 특정한 과업에 맞는 전략을 선택적으로 사용하지 않고 무작위로 사용하기 때문에 효율성이 떨어진다. 즉, 전략 기반 수업을 토대로 비효율적 학습을 하는 학습자에게 특정한 과업에 필요한 전략을 명확히 가르침으로써 보다 성공적인 학습을 해나갈 수 있도록 해야 한다.

① 초인지적 전략(metacognitive strategy): 제2언어 학습과 직접적인 관련이 없으나, 성공적인 언어 학습을 이루기 위한 학습자의 제2언어 단계별 학습 계획이나 제2언어 사용 중 자신의 발화와 이해에 대한 모니터 및 전체적인 학습 후 성공도에 대한 평가를 할 때 갖는 전략이다.

Metacognitive strategies involve high-order strategies and make use of knowledge about cognitive process by means of analyzing, monitoring, evaluating, planning, and organizing one's own learning process.

 **In the Classroom** |||||||||||||||||||||||||||||||||||||||||||||||||||||||||||||||||||||||||||||||||||||||||||||||

Case 1

In today's English class, Minji and her partner were asked to read a newspaper article and retell the story to each other. Their performance was video-recorded. Minji wrote the following in her learning log after watching the video.

Minji's Learning Log

Mistakes and difficulties I had during the task

The newspaper article had a lot of new words that I've never seen before. I was worried if I could accurately retell the story.

Strategies I used to complete the task

Since I didn't have time to look up words in the dictionary, I had to guess their meanings based on the context. I thought I understood the story. When I didn't have enough words to describe it, I simply used Korean words.

Overall assessment of my performance on today's task

I paused a lot without speaking while I was telling the story because I didn't know what to say in English. When I was listening, I didn't understand my partner's story clearly. But I didn't ask her to repeat it because I wasn't sure if it was okay.

Strategies I will practice

In the past, I wrote down new words at least ten times to memorize them. It didn't work very well, but I don't know how else I can remember the words. I will try to read more so I can learn more new words.

Case 2: Think Aloud Technique

To investigate learner strategies, teachers can let learners think aloud as thinking processes or strategies they are making use of. For example, while writing a composition, a student may record his or her thoughts into a tape recorder during the planning, drafting, and revision of the composition. Later, the recording may be used to determine the planning or revision processes used by the student.

T: Today, we are going to work on a learning strategy. Learning this strategy will improve our comprehension and the speed at which we read. Well, I'm going to hand out a reading passage. Let us listen in.

What I do first is read the title. I try to figure out what the passage is about. I look at the subheadings and pictures, too, if there are any. I ask myself what I know about the topic and what questions I have. Next, I read the first paragraph. I don't read every word, however, I let my eyes skim it very quickly—just picking out what I think are the main ideas. I especially look at the content or meaning—bearing words—usually the nouns and verbs.

➡ 교사가 자신의 읽기 과정(thinking process)을 소리 내 단계적으로 제시하고 있다.

Complete the following table after reading the text.

What did you do during reading?				
	Not very much	A little bit	Much of the time	All of the time
made prediction		√		
formed pictures	√			
used analogy		√		
found problem		√		
used fixed-ups			√	

➡ 학생이 사용한 읽기 과정을 체크리스트에 표시함으로써 자신의 전략을 파악할 수 있다.

② 인지적 전략(cognitive strategy): 외국어 학습 과제를 수행할 때 사용하는 구체적인 전략으로, 학습 과제 및 자료를 직접 조작해 어떻게 받아들일 것인가에 관련된 기능이다.

Cognitive strategies are thought processes used *directly* in learning which enable learners to deal with the information presented in tasks and materials by working on it in different ways.

Cognitive strategies are one type of learning strategy that learners use in order to learn more successfully. These include repetition, organizing new language, summarizing meaning, guessing meaning from context, using imagery for memorization. All of these strategies involve deliberate manipulation of language to improve learning.

Ex : A learner remembers new words by visualizing them represented in a memorable or ridiculous situation. This makes it easier and faster to recall these words.

In the classroom, activities which can be described as cognitive strategies include making mind maps, visualization, association, mnemonics, using clues in reading comprehension, underlining key words, scanning, skimming and inferencing.

③ 사회정의적 전략(socio-affective strategy): 학습 과정에서 일어나는 사회적 활동이나 상호작용에서 사용하는 전략이다. Social strategy는 상호작용을 통해 의사소통의 기회를 증진시키는 전략을, affective strategy는 성공적인 학습과 과제 해결을 위해 정서적인 요인을 조절하는 전략을 말한다.

Affective strategies, such as identifying one's mood and anxiety level, talking about feelings, rewarding oneself for good performance, and using deep breathing or positive self-talk, have been shown to be significantly related to L2 proficiency. *Social strategies* (e.g. asking questions to get verification, asking for clarification of a confusing point, asking for help in doing a language task, talking with a native-speaking conversation partner, and exploring cultural and social norms) help the learner work with others and understand the target culture as well as the language. Social strategies were significantly associated with L2 proficiency.

🧑‍🏫 In the Classroom

Level : Intermediate

Time : 50 minutes

Aim : For students to improve their reading by learning to preview and to skim to get the gist of a reading passage

Teaching Procedure

Step 1: Learning journals & Interview

Prior to the lesson the teacher has been reading the students' learning journals, where the students regularly write about what and how they are learning. The teacher has also been interviewing the students.

Step 2: Decision of the strategy of advance organization

The teacher decides to have students work on the strategy of advance organization. He thinks that they need to improve their reading by preview and to skim to get the gist of a reading passage; Learning this strategy will improve their comprehension and the speed at which they read.

Step 3: The teacher models the use of the strategy using a think–aloud demonstration.

He begins the class with a presentation. He tells students that they are going to work on a learning strategy called advance organization. He begins by modelling. He distributed a reading passage.

'What I do first is reading the title. I try to figure out what the passage is about. I look at the subheadings and pictures, too, if there are any. I ask myself what I know about the topic and what questions I have. Next, I read the first paragraph. I don't read every word, however. I let my eyes skim it very quickly—just picking out what I think are the main ideas. I especially look at the content or meaning—bearing words—usually the nouns and verbs.'

The teacher calls out the words that he considers key in the first paragraph. 'From doing these things, I know that this passage is about wild horses. I do not know very much about the topic, but from skimming the first paragraph, I have gotten the impression that the passage is about the challenges of catching and taming wild horses.'

Step 4: The students practice the new learning strategy.

'I'd like you to practice just this much now. I am going to hand out a new reading passage for you to practice on. When you get it, keep it face down. Don't read it yet. Does everyone have one? Good. Now remember, before you turn the paper over, you are going to be practicing the strategy that I have just introduced. Ready? Turn over the paper. Take a look. Now quickly turn it face down again. What do you think that this passage is about? Who can guess?'

One student says he thinks that it is about whales. 'Why do you think so?' asks the teacher. The student says he has guessed from the title, which is 'Rescuing the World's Largest Mammal.' 'What do you think is meant by "rescuing"?' the teacher asks, No one knows so the teacher asks them to keep this question in mind as they read.

'Turn your page over again. Read through the first paragraph quickly. Do not read every word. Skip those you don't know the meaning of. Do not use your dictionary.' The teacher gives the students two minutes to read the first paragraph.

He then asks, 'Who can tell us what the main idea of the passage is—what is the gist?' A student replies that the passage is about certain types of whales being put on the endangered list. 'That's a good guess' says the teacher.

Step 5: The students evaluate their own success in learning the strategy. They modify the strategy to meet their own learning needs.

Next the students evaluate how they have done. Some feel distressed because they still feel that they need to understand every word. However, others are feeling better because they realize that their reading assignments need not take as long as they have been taking. Some students discuss their implementation of the strategy and how they modified it. All of the students feel that they need a lot more practice with this new strategy.

Step 6: The teacher asks the students to try out the new strategy on a different reading they choose for homework that night.

➡ 위에 제시된 학습 전략은 학생들의 외국어 학습에 도움이 되며, 목표 언어 및 학습 방법도 함께 습득함으로써 학생들은 보다 독립적이고 자기주도적인 학습을 해 나갈 수 있다. 또한 자기 평가(self-assessment)를 통해 학습자 자율성(learner autonomy)을 키워 나갈 수 있다. 즉, 본 학습 전략은 개인마다 직접적인 방법으로 훈련하는 것이 가장 효율적이다 (with 'hands-on' experience).

Further Reading

성인이 아동보다 언어 학습에서 유리하다는 견해가 있다. 성인은 성공적인 학습에 중요한 의식적인 학습과 무의식적인 학습 방법을 모두 취할 수 있기 때문이다. 학습은 편안한 상태에서 자연스럽게 일어나기도 하지만 의도적으로 자신이 사용하는 언어를 점검하고, 보다 나은 언어 사용을 위해 전략 학습이 필요한 순간도 있다. 즉, 언어 수업에서 진행되는 말하기, 읽기, 어휘, 듣기 및 쓰기 활동을 하기 위해 학습자들은 필요한 언어 학습 전략을 사용한다: metacognitive, cognitive and compensation strategies

Recognizing that there is a task to complete or a problem to solve, language learners will use whatever metacognitive, cognitive or social/affective strategies they possess to attend to the language-learning activity. This is done consciously.

1. **Direct Strategies**: mental processing of the language
   ① **Memory Strategies**: to store and retrieve new information
   ② **Cognitive Strategies**: to help learners to understand and produce new language through a series of means such as summarizing and reasoning, among others
   ③ **Compensation Strategies**: When learners feel they have certain limitations in getting their messages through or in understanding what other people are telling them, they make use of the compensation strategies to fill in the gaps in communication, like making intelligent guesses, asking for clarification, asking for repetition, and so forth.

2. **Indirect Strategies**: "support and manage language learning without involving the target language."
   ① **Metacognitive Strategies**: to allow learners take control of their own knowledge by using functions such as centering, arranging, planning and evaluating. Since learners get very confused with all of the rules, vocabulary, and writing systems when learning a new language, they get hold of the metacognitive strategies to reorganize their schemata or previous knowledge and overview and link new material with old material.
   ② **Affective Strategies**: to deal with emotions, attitudes, motivations and values. Krashen (1988) has highlighted the need to foster a low affective filter in language learning since it is one of the biggest influences on language learning success or failure. Positive emotions and attitudes are accomplished through the affective strategies when learners are engaged in relaxation activities, when they are involved in music and laughter, when they take risks wisely and are self-rewarded, or when they take their own emotional temperature and realize when they are anxious by doing checklists, writing a language learning diary or by discussing their feelings.

연구에 따르면, 언어 학습자는 성공적인 학습과 언어 수행을 향상시킬 수 있는 방법에 대한 효율적인 전략 기반 수업을 받아야 한다. 전략 기반 수업은 uninformed instruction과 direct and integrated instruction의 두 가지 방법이 제시되고 있다. Uninformed instruction은 학생들이 과업과 자료를 통해 특정한 전략을 사용해 보도록 하는 것으로, 학습되는 전략에 대한 명칭이나 목적 등이 명시적으로 제시되지 않는다. 반면, direct and integrated instruction은 다음과 같다.

Direct and integrated instruction informs learners of the value and purpose of learning strategies and helps learners to use, identify and develop learning strategies in a systematic way as they learn the target language.

The teacher explains to the learners the value, importance and purpose for strategy use to raise awareness in the application of these strategies, to make them identify specific strategies for specific tasks, and to provide opportunities for reflection, practice, and self-evaluation. Through this direct and integrated approach to strategy instruction learners become reactive learners as they increase their awareness, practice, use and monitoring of the language learning strategies they are using while learning a second or foreign language.

When learners practice using the direct strategies, they are involved in activities when they create mental linkages, apply images and sounds, review material, employ action (**memory strategies**). They also practice through repeating, recognition of formulas and patterns, recombining, and practicing naturalistically, as well as receiving and sending messages, analyzing and reasoning, and creating structure for input and output (**cognitive strategies**). Added to these activities, language learners start using linguistic cues to make intelligent guesses and get the message through; they ask for help; they use mimes and gestures, and so forth (**compensation strategies**).

Indirect strategy use instruction facilitates learners in centering their own learning by linking new material to already known material, by paying more attention to specific details, and by delaying production and focusing more on comprehension or the training of their listening skills. Learners start organizing more and identifying the focus of the task they have to accomplish. They get more involved in group work activities since they start seeking for more practice opportunities. Learners become aware of what they are doing and self-monitor and self-evaluate (**metacognitive strategies**). If they are anxious and feel fear in the performance of tasks, they start taking risks because they understand that learning is a process of making errors and overcoming them. So, they write their problems, they discuss them in class, and they view language learning as a positive and rewarding experience (**affective strategies**). Since learners are instructed in pair and group work too when they are involved in strategy training, they cooperate more with peers as well as with proficient users of the language. Empathy is triggered and there's a development of cultural understanding. Language learners feel the need for supporting one another and are aware of the thoughts and feelings of other. There's also a greater use of the functions of the language and feedback on errors is greatly accomplished (**social strategies**).

(2) Communication Strategies

① **Avoidance Strategies**: Avoidance is a tactic for preventing a pitfall, a linguistic weakness that could break down communicative flow. Syntactic, phonological, and lexical avoidance are common tactics in successful learners, as is topic avoidance. Psychologically, avoidance is a combination of face-saving and maintaining communicative interaction.

ⓐ 어휘적 회피: 자신의 제2언어 활용 능력의 부족으로 어휘가 떠오르지 않을 경우에 사용한다.

> Ex L : I lost my road.
> NS : You lost your road?
> L : ... I lost. I lost. I got lost.

ⓑ 음운적 회피: 발음과 같은 음운적 어려움이 생길 때 사용한다.

> Ex L : My uncle is selling his boat.
> NS : He is sailing his boat?
> L : Sell not sail.
>   ⋮
> L : Somebody will buy his boat.

ⓒ 통사적 & 주제 회피: 자신의 제2언어 능력으로 감당하기 어려운 주제에 직면했을 경우에 사용한다.

> Ex NS : Let's talk about your recent trip!
> L : (silence)

② **Compensatory Strategies**

ⓐ 조립식 문형(prefabricated pattern): 초보자들이 주로 사용하며, 흔히 사용되는 구 또는 문장을 통째로 암기하는 경우이다.

Using memorized stock phrases usually for "survival" purpose.

> Ex How much does this cost?
> Where is the toilet?

ⓑ 도움 요청(appeal for help, appeal to authority): 의사소통의 문제가 있을 때 즉각적으로 도움을 요청하는 경우이다.

Asking for aid from the interlocutor directly.

> **Ex** What do you call X in English?

ⓒ 언어 전환(code-switching): 제2언어로는 표현하기 어려운 부분을 자신이 알고 있는 제1언어 또는 제3언어로 사용하는 경우이다.

Using a L1 word with L1 pronunciation or a L3 word with L3 pronunciation while speaking in L2.

> **Ex❶** I want to have 점심.

> **Ex❷** S1: What did you do in your summer vacation?
> S2: I went to 시골집 in which my grandparents have lived.
> S1: Wow, I bet you had great time there.
> S2: Absolutely.

ⓓ 우회적 표현(circumlocution): 학습자가 전하고자 하는 내용을 돌려서 표현하는 경우이다.

Describing or providing examples of the target object or actions.

> **Ex** S1: There aren't many kids in my neighborhood, so my younger sister doesn't have anyone to play with.
> S2: (When the word, 'pet' didn't come to S2's mind) Maybe, she needs a, a, *a dog or a cat to play with, some kind of animal.*

ⓔ 유사어 사용(approximation): 나타내고자 하는 표현과 유사한 언어를 사용하는 경우이다.

Using an alternative term which expresses the meaning of the target lexical item as closely as possible.

> **Ex** S1: Can I borrow your *ship?*
> S2: I see. You mean the *sailboat*, don't you?

ⓕ 조어(word coinage): 학습자 나름의 규칙에 의해 존재하지 않는 표현을 생성하는 경우이다.

Creating a nonexisting L2 word based on a supposed rule.

> **Ex** vegetarianist for vegetarian

ⓖ 비언어적 표현(nonlinguistic signals): 얼굴표현, 동작 및 행동을 통해 의미를 전달하는 경우이다. (mime, gesture, facial expression)

> **Ex** Guest: I need, you know the thing. I do this (*gestures brushing her hair and blow-drying it*) after I and washing my hair.

ⓗ 직역(literal translation): 제2언어를 모국어로 그대로 직역해 표현하는 경우이다.

> **Ex** *pig meat* for pork

ⓘ 시간 끌기(stalling or time-gaining strategies, keeping the floor): well, let's see, now 등의 시간을 벌기 위한 표현이다.

ⓙ 외국어화(foreignizing): 모국어를 마치 외국어 방식으로 발음하거나 모국어에 외국어 접미사를 붙여 의사소통을 하는 경우이다.

> **Ex** 유아tic

Further Reading

Types of CSs

Communication strategies have five main categories and a number of subcategories which add up the following list:

1. Paraphrase

Paraphrase includes three subcategories which are:

① **Approximation:** The use of such native language(L1) vocabulary items or structures, that the language learner is aware of not being correct, but which shares certain semantic features with the desired item, thus satisfying the speaker's intention (e.g. a big rock instead of boulder, or pipe instead of water pipe).

② **Word Coinage:** The learner is making up a new word—most often on the spot—in order to communicate a desired concept (e.g. airball for balloon or smoking leaf for cigar).

③ **Circumlocution:** The learner describes the major characteristics or elements of an object, action or person instead of using the target language(TL) equivalent (e.g. She is, uh, smoking something. I don't know what's its name. That's, uh, Cuban, and they smoke it in other countries, too).

2. Transfer

Transfer has two subcategories that are:

① **Literal Translation**: The learner is translating word for word from L1 to L2 (e.g. He invites him to drink. replacing They toast one another.).

② **Language Switch**: The learner uses the L1 term without bothering to translate it into L2 (e.g. léggömb instead of balloon or Verkehrsmittel replacing means of transport).

3. Appeal for Assistance

This refers to the learner asking for the correct term or structure from an exterior source of information, most likely a teacher or a fellow student (e.g. What is this? or How do you call that in English?).

4. Mime

Mime is related to the speaker using non-verbal strategies substituting an expression (e.g. clapping one's hands to illustrate applause, or rubbing one's eyes to indicate crying or tiredness, boredom).

5. Avoidance

Avoidance consists of two subcategories outlined below:

① **Topic Avoidance**: The language learner is omitting concepts for which his/her vocabulary is lacking at the time of speaking.

② **Message Abandonment**: The language user begins to talk about a concept but being completely unable to continue doing so due to a lack of phrases and expressions and thus ends up stopping in the middle of an utterance.

02 \ 정의적 요인(Affective Domain)

1 Motivation

(1) 개념

동기란 특정 행동을 유발하고 유지시키는 욕구 및 감정을 말한다.

① 통합적 동기(integrative motivation): 목표 문화에 통합돼 사회적 일원이 되고자 하는 욕구에 의한 동기

Integrative motivation is based on interest in learning L2 because of a desire to learn about or associate with the people who use it or an intention to participate or integrate in the L2-using speech community.

② 도구적 동기(instrumental motivation): 목표 문화나 언어가 아닌 다른 목적을 위한 자신의 필요성에 의한 동기

Instrumental motivation involves perception of purely practical value in learning the L2 such as increasing occupational opportunities, enhancing prestige, or just passing a course in school.

③ 내적 동기(intrinsic motivation): 내적 보상에 의한 언어 학습

Learners are studying because they want to do it or they have made their own choice to learn. They don't need a reward from someone else to do well.

④ 외적 동기(extrinsic motivation): 외적 보상에 의한 언어 학습

External motivation is when other influences such as teachers or school requirements, push learners to study L2. In this case, learners often need to receive rewards such as good grades, high scores, and praise. Without rewards, you may not be motivated enough to study L2 very hard.

Actually, integrative and instrumental motivations are not necessarily mutually exclusive. It is stated that learners rarely select only one type of motivation when learning a second language. The motivation of learning a second language is usually a combination of different forms of orientations. Take an example of international students who are residents in the United States. The international students learn English for academic purposes while wishing to be integrated with the people and culture of the country at the same time. This example has clearly shown that integrative and instrumental motivations can mutually exist. In some cases, it is difficult to divide instrumental and integrative motivations.

Plus ➕

Different Types of Motivations

Types	Integrative	Instrumental
Extrinsic	It will enable me to travel all over the world and get many friends while communicating with people from other countries.	I take English to pass an entrance exam.
Intrinsic	It will enable me to gain good friends more easily among English speaking people, and make me feel happy.	It will enable me to read and listen to English language media for information and pleasure.

(2) 학습과의 관계

동기와 태도는 다양한 학습자들의 외국어 숙달 정도를 결정하는 중요한 요인이다. 따라서, 외국어 학습에 대한 동기가 높은 학습자일수록 빠르고 성공적인 학습 결과를 보인다.

Individuals who are motivated will learn another language faster and to a greater degree. And some degree of motivation is involved in initial decisions to learn and maintain learning. Furthermore, motivation is a predictor of language-learning success.

(3) 내적 동기 유발 방법

교사는 학생들이 교실 수업에서 자기 보상을 찾을 수 있도록, 흥미롭고 의미 있으며 도전적인 과제를 제공해 그들의 내적 동기를 유발시켜 성공적인 외국어 학습에 이르도록 도와줘야 한다.

① 교사는 외적 보상자로서의 역할이 아니라, 학습자 스스로 학습할 수 있도록 돕는 안내자의 역할을 담당하기 때문에 의사소통 언어 교수에서 교사의 역할은 facilitator와 resource person으로 명명된다.

Teachers are enablers, not rewarders.

② 학습자는 교사에게 의존적인 학습을 하지 않고, 자율성을 키워 자기주도적인 학습을 해 나간다. 학습자 스스로 학습을 계획하고 관리하고 평가하며 자신의 학습에 대한 책임감과 주도성을 키우도록 한다.

Learners need to develop autonomy, not dependence.

Ex 학습 일지(learning log) 등을 작성하게 한다.

③ 학습자가 학습 전략과 개인적인 목표를 통해 학습을 주체적으로 수행할 수 있도록 돕는다.

Help learners to take charge of their own learning through setting some personal goals and utilizing learning strategies.

④ 학습자 중심 및 협동적인 교수가 내적 동기를 극대화시킨다. 경쟁적인 학습 활동을 지양하고 학습자들에 의한 학습 자료 구성 및 과업 활동을 준비하도록 한다.

Learner-centered, cooperative teaching is intrinsically motivating.

⑤ 내용 기반 수업 활동과 수업 과정이 내적 동기를 극대화시킨다. 학습자들의 실생활과 학습 목적에 부합하는 topic 및 content를 선택하도록 한다.

Content-based activities and courses are intrinsically motivating.

⑥ 교사의 세심한 배려에 의한 평가(essay feedback 등)가 학습자들의 학습을 내적 동기화시키고, 학습자의 현재 학습에 대한 평가와 개선을 위한 평가 도구, comment를 제공한다. Classroom testing에 대한 평가 방식으로 analytic scoring을 제시해 학습자의 strength와 weakness를 진단한 뒤 further study에 반영할 수 있도록 한다.

Test, with some special attention from the teacher, can be intrinsically motivating.

Plus ⊕

How to Maintain Student's Motivation in Class (1)

1. The content needs to be relevant to their age and level of ability, and the learning goals need to be challenging yet manageable and clear.
2. Varying the activities, tasks, and materials to increase student's interest levels.
3. Using cooperative rather than competitive goals to increase students' self-confidence.

How to Maintain Student's Motivation in Class (2)

성공적인 학습을 위해서는 질 좋은 수업과 언어적 입력, 상호작용 및 실질적인 언어 사용의 기회 등이 필요하지만, 학습자들의 언어 학습에 대한 동기 또한 매우 중요하다. 따라서 내적 동기를 토대로 외적 동기를 키워줌으로써 성공적인 언어 학습을 이룰 수 있도록 해야 한다.

Learners need quality instruction, input, interaction, and opportunities for meaningful output, not only to make progress, but also to maintain motivation for language learning. A good teacher, then, must tap into the sources of intrinsic motivation and find ways to connect them with external motivational factors that can be brought to a classroom setting. This is especially significant when English is not seen as important to the students' immediate needs, other than to pass exams. Because learners have different purposes for studying a language, it is important for instructors to identify students' purposes and needs and to develop proper motivational strategies. Students should understand why they need to make an effort, how long they must sustain an activity, how hard they should pursue it, and how motivated they feel toward their pursuits.

➡ 교실 수업 중 학생들의 동기를 유지하는 것은 매우 어렵다. 따라서 다음과 같은 전략 등이 도움이 될 수 있을 것이다.

1. **Create a friendly atmosphere in the classroom.**

   Develop a friendly climate in which all students feel recognized and valued. Many students feel more comfortable participating in classroom activities after they know their teacher and their peers. Creating a safe and comfortable environment where everyone feels like a part of the whole is one of the most significant factors in encouraging motivation. Doing so may take time as students adjust themselves to a new setting.

   Ex ┆ At the beginning of the school year, you can provide students with a bright and colorful classroom with pictures and projects completed by the previous year's students. This gives students the impression that learning the target language will be easy and enjoyable. It also gives students a chance to learn from what is present in the environment. Pair and group activities can be used from the very outset, reducing the pressure of teacher-student interaction and allowing students to feel recognized by their peers. The feeling of becoming a part of the whole is one of the strongest motivational factors at the beginning of a school year.

One ice-breaker that you could use to start this process is the nickname activity. Students can invent and write down a nickname (or use a nickname they already have). Arranged in a circle, each student has to stand up and explain his or her nickname. Along with introducing themselves, this fun activity gives students a chance to create a friendly and flexible classroom atmosphere.

2. Encourage students to personalize the classroom environment.

Providing students with a learner-centered, low-anxiety classroom environment has a great impact on language acquisition. Personalizing the environment can relax the students and enhance the friendly atmosphere, which will increase their desire to learn and develop their language skills. Students who feel safe and comfortable will feel more secure taking chances; they will display greater motivation to read aloud in class or write an essay without the fear of being criticized.

> Ex : I remember very well, as a student, my English teacher giving us a chance to arrange the classroom in the way that would make us feel most comfortable. The teacher gave us the impression that there was no limit to what we could do to our learning environment. We covered the walls with colorful movie posters and the lyrics of famous songs, and we also personalized our desks. Our classroom became a warm, cheerful place where we enjoyed learning and studying.

3. Create situations in which students will feel a sense of accomplishment.

A sense of accomplishment is a great factor in motivating students. Be sure to give positive feedback and reinforcement. Doing so can increase students' satisfaction and encourage positive self-evaluation. A student who feels a sense of accomplishment will be better able to direct his or her own studies and learning outcomes. Positive as well as negative comments influence motivation, but research consistently indicates that students are more affected by positive feedback and success. Praise builds students' self-confidence, competence, and self-esteem.

However, giving positive feedback should not be mistaken for correcting mistakes without giving explanations. Some teachers correct students' mistakes without really explaining the reason for doing so. It is very important for teachers to point out the good aspects of a student's work and to provide a clear explanation of his or her mistakes. Students value the teacher's ideas when they feel that their good work is appreciated, and this encourages them to start evaluating themselves for further studies.

4. Encourage students to set their own short-term goals.

Language learners can achieve success by setting their own goals and by directing their studies toward their own expectations. Students can help themselves achieve their goals by determining their own language needs and by defining why they want to learn the language. Having goals and expectations leads to increased motivation, which in turn leads to a higher level of language competence. We as teachers should encourage students to have specific short-term goals such as communicating with English speakers or reading books in English. No matter what these goals are, we should help students set and pursue them.

5. Provide pair and group activities to develop students' confidence.

Students learn by doing, making, writing, designing, creating, and solving. Passivity decreases students' motivation and curiosity. Students' enthusiasm, involvement, and willingness to participate affect the quality of class discussion as an opportunity for learning. Small-group activities and pair work boost students' self-confidence and are excellent sources of motivation. Group work can give quiet students a chance to express their ideas and feelings on a topic because they find it easier to speak to groups of three or four than to an entire class. Once students have spoken in small groups, they usually become less reluctant to speak to the class as a whole. Group activities allow students not only to express their ideas but also to work cooperatively, which increases class cohesion and thus motivation.

> **Ex** ｜ I often do a vocabulary exercise in which I put students in groups of four. I distribute vocabulary words on flashcards, and each student must choose one of the flashcards without showing the word to fellow group members. Then, each student explains his or her word by giving three clues to the group without using the actual word. Using the clues, the other students must draw pictures that reflect the meaning of the word. This activity gives students flexibility to use other skills for their language development. It also gives quieter students a chance to express themselves within their groups, even when they are not confident to express themselves in front of the entire class.

6. Connect language learning to students' interests outside of class.

In today's high-tech learning environment, it would be unfair to limit students to traditional methods. Encouraging students to relate their classroom experience to outside interests and activities makes developing language skills more relevant. For example, computer-assisted language learning could be linked to playing computer games, or to computer programs that the students are interested in using. Listening to English language songs, watching English language films or videos, and reading English language Web sites can lead students to broaden their perspective on their language acquisition process.

Motivational teaching strategies such as these can easily increase language learners' motivation levels. The idea that student motivation is a personality trait and that students are either motivated or unmotivated is incorrect. Without sufficient motivation, even individuals with the most remarkable abilities cannot achieve their long-term goals. As instructors, we may be the most important factor in influencing our students' motivation, which is a key element in the language acquisition process.

2 Self Confidence(Self-esteem)

자신과 자신의 능력에 대한 자신감은 제2언어 습득에서 중요한 요소로, 방어기제(inhibition)와 위험 감수(risk-taking), 긴장감(anxiety) 등과 영향을 주고받는다.

Self-esteem refers to the degree to which individuals feel confident and believe themselves to be significant people. Closely related to the notion of self-esteem is the concept of inhibition and language ego, risk-taking, anxiety, empathy and so on.

(1) Inhibition & Language Ego

학습자는 외국어 학습 시 자신감과 자아를 보호하기 위한 수단으로 억압(inhibition)이라는 방어기제를 사용한다. 이때 학습자의 보다 효과적인 언어 습득을 위해서는 억압의 기제를 적절한 수준으로 낮춰야 하는데, 이를 위해 교사는 수업 중 guessing game 혹은 communication game을 진행할 수 있다.

The extent to which individuals build defences to protect their egos. People vary in how adaptive their language egos are, i.e., how able they are to deal with the identity conflict involved in L2 learning. When people began to speak their native language, they have learned to understand themselves in their own language. The close connection between language and ego is called language ego: the way language helps you to understand and express yourself.

> ▶ **Willingness to communicate**: An underlying continuum representing the predisposition toward or away from communicating, given the choice. Or, more simply put, "the intention to initiate communication, given a choice."

Plus ⊕

How to Lower Inhibition

1. to play guessing games and communication games
2. to do role-play and skits
3. to sing songs
4. to use plenty of group works
5. to laugh with your students
6. to have students share their fears in small groups

(2) Anxiety

긴장감에는 언어 습득을 촉진하는 facilitative anxiety와 학습을 저해하는 debilitative anxiety가 있다. 교사는 학습을 저해하는 불안감이나 초조함 등은 없애고, 경쟁심 등을 자극해 학습을 촉진하는 긴장감을 활용하도록 한다.

Learner anxiety is the feeling of worry, nervousness, and stress. Anxiety is not always a negative factor in learning like many other factors.

① *Facilitative (helpful) anxiety* motivates learners to fight the new learning task, prompting them to make extra efforts to overcome their feelings of anxiety.

② *Debilitative (harmful) anxiety* causes the learners to flee the learning task in order to avoid the source of anxiety.

③ **Trait anxiety**: At the deepest, or global level, trait anxiety is a more permanent predisposition to be anxious.

④ **State anxiety**: At a more momentary, or situational level, state anxiety is experienced in relation to some particular event or act.

(3) Risk-taking

Risk-taking이란 오류를 범할 수 있는 약간의 모험을 감수하며 언어를 사용하는 것을 말하는데, 적절한 수준의 위험 감수는 성공적인 학습에 큰 영향을 끼친다. 교사는 Risk-taking을 위한 수업 분위기 조성을 위해 자발적 추측을 장려하고 유창성에 초점을 둔 활동을 많이 활용하도록 한다.

Risk-taking is an important characteristic of successful second language acquisition. Learners have to be able to gamble a bit to be willing to try out hunches about the language and take the risk of being wrong. Risk-takers show less hesitancy, are more willing to use complex language, and are more tolerant of errors. The concepts of risk-taking, anxiety, and extroversion would appear to be related, as would those of self-esteem and inhibition.

(4) Extroversion & Introversion

외향성(extroversion)은 타인으로부터 만족감이나 자긍심을 얻어내려는 성향으로서 말하기와 의사소통 능력에 유리하며, 내향성(introversion)은 자아로부터 이를 얻어내려는 성향으로서 자기 발견적 학습과 읽기 수업에 능하다.

Extroversion is the extent to which a person has a deep-seated need to receive ego enhancement and self-esteem from others. On the other hand, *introversion* is the extent to which a person derives a sense of wholeness and fulfillment apart from a reflection of this self from other people. Extroverts are sociable, risk-taking, lively, and active; introverts are quiet and prefer non-sociable activities.

By definition, extroverts gain their greatest energy from the external world. They want interaction with people and have many friendships, some deep and some not. In contrast, introverts derive their energy from the internal world, seeking solitude and tending to have just a few friendships, which are often very deep. Extroverts and introverts can learn to work together with the help of the teacher. Enforcing time limits in the L2 classroom can keep extroverts' enthusiasm to a manageable level. Rotating the person in charge of leading L2 discussions gives introverts the opportunity to participate equally with extroverts.

(5) Empathy

감정이입(empathy)이란 자신의 자아를 뛰어넘어 타인을 이해하는 과정으로, '언어'를 감정이입 과정의 중요한 수단으로 삼는다. 감정이입이 뛰어난 학습자는 협동 학습과 상호작용적 수업에 능하기 때문에 원어민으로부터 진정성 있는 발음을 용이하게 습득할 수 있다.

Empathy concerns the ability to put oneself in the position of another person in order to understand him or her better.

기출 엿보기   2009학년도

(1) Jin-soo is a high school student learning English in Korea. For him, studying and learning English does not feel like a burden. He likes to receive and produce English whenever he can. In addition, he feels that learning English is important because it will allow him to converse and be with various international speakers of English.

(2) Hye-ri is a university student who is learning English in Korea. She is taking a course in English literature taught by a Canadian professor. Even though she sometimes does not understand everything that the professor says in the lectures, it does not bother her. During her group study meetings with her classmates, she feels nervous when she speaks in English but tries to speak whenever she can. She wants to do well in English because it is important for her to show her ability to her family and friends.

(3) Mi-jin is an office worker and she is presently studying English in Australia for a period of six months. She is taking an English class at a language institute there. For Mi-jin learning English is important because she thinks that it will add to her social status back in Korea. In relation to classroom activities at the institute, she enjoys participating in small group speaking activities, particularly jigsaw tasks. The high level of challenge presented by the tasks makes her feel nervous, but this tension pushes her to do well in them. Concerning the reading activities, she doesn't like reading something in English because she feels that she should always look up unfamiliar words in a dictionary.

➡ a. Jin-soo is both intrinsically and integratively motivated.
  b. Hye-ri is extrinsically motivated and engages in risk-taking behavior.
  c. Mi-jin is extrinsically motivated and has a high willingness to communicate.
  d. Mi-jin experiences facilitative anxiety, and she has a low tolerance of ambiguity when reading.

Plus ➕

1. Learning Style Taxonomy for the L2 Classroom

Type 1: Cognitive Styles	Type 2: Sensory Styles	Type 3: Personality Styles
• **Field Dependent** learns best when information is presented in context. They are often more fluent language learners. • **Field Independent** learns most effectively step-by-step and with sequential instruction. They are often more accurate language learners.	Perceptual: • **Visual** learns best when there is visual reinforcement such as charts, pictures, graphs, etc. • **Auditory** learns more effectively by listening to information. • **Tactile** learns more effectively when there is an opportunity to use manipulative resources. • **Kinesthetic** learns more effectively when there is movement associated with learning.	**Tolerance of Ambiguity** refers to how comfortable a learner is with uncertainty; some students do well in situations where there are several possible answers; others prefer one correct answer.

• **Analytic** works more effectively alone and at his/her own pace. • **Global** works more effectively in groups.	Environmental: • **Physical** sensitive to learning environment, such as light, temperature, furniture. • **Sociological** sensitive to relationships within the learning environment.	Right and Left Hemisphere Dominance: • **Left-brain** dominant learners tend to be more visual, analytical, reflective, and self-reliant. • **Right-brain** dominant learners tend to be more anditory, global, impulsive, and interactive.
• **Reflective** learns more effectively when they have time to consider new information before responding. • **Impulsive** learns more effectively when they can respond to new information immediately; as language learners, they are risk takers.		

2. Agency in Language Classroom

Anticipated material and social outcomes are not the only reward influencing human behavior. Agency motivates, monitors, and regulates individuals' execution of decision made and actions planned. People exercise self-direction keeping in mind personal standards and regulate their behaviors by self-evaluative outcomes. Agency also enables individuals to examine their metacognitive capability to reflect on the adequacy of one's thoughts and actions. Agency can be exercised not only directly by an individual but also by proxy or collectively.

① Encourage Learners to *Do* Language.
② Allow Learners' *Voice* to Develop.
③ Promote Perceptual Learning and Affordances.
④ Guide Students to Develop Self-Regulating Strategies.

03 사회문화적 요인(Sociocultural Factor)

1 Acculturation Model

문화 변용(acculturation)이란 제2언어 학습과 함께 습득하게 되는 제2언어의 문화와 제2의 정체성(identity)을 통한 문화 동화를 뜻한다. 이때 문화 변용에 가장 큰 영향을 끼치는 요인으로는 사회적 거리감(social distance)과 심리적 거리감(psychological distance)이 있다.

Acculturation means the process of becoming adapted to a new culture. According to Acculturation Model, second language learning involves the acquisition of a second identity and requires learning the culture of that community and adapting to those values and behavioral patterns. The extent to which learners acculturate depends on two sets of factors: social distance and psychological distance, which limit acculturation, and thus inhibit L2 learning

(1) Social Distance

the cognitive and affective proximity of two cultures that come into contact within an individual

(2) Psychological Distance

the extent to which individual learners are comfortable with the learning task, therefore, a personal rather than a group dimension

② 문화 변용의 단계

(1) 흥분과 행복감(Excitement & Euphoria)

a period of excitement and euphoria over the newness of the surroundings

(2) 문화 충격(Culture Shock)

자신의 문화와 목표 문화 간의 차이를 인식한다.

Individuals feel the intrusion of more and more cultural differences into their own images of self and security.

(3) 문화 압력(Culture Stress)

문화 충격이 점진적으로 회복되면서 겪는 문화적 긴장의 단계로, 초기에 아노미(anomie, cultural homeless) 현상을 겪는다.

(4) 문화 동화(Acculturation)

문화 충격에서 완전히 회복해 목표 문화에 동화되고 제2의 자아를 갖게 된다.

Near or full recovery either, assimilation or adaptation, acceptance of the new culture and self-confidence in the "new" person that has developed in this culture.

3 Teaching Culture

(1) E-mail Survey

Students communicate with their target language counterparts and investigate information about their daily routines, school, and interests and compare these data to their own responses.

(2) Culture Capsules

Students hear a brief description that illustrates a difference between Korean culture and the target culture, discuss the difference, perform role plays based on the ideas, and integrate this information into activities that incorporate other skills.

① A culture capsule consists of a paragraph or so of explanation of one minimal difference between an American and a target custom, along with several illustrative photos or relevant realia.

② Culture capsules are a brief description of and aspect of the target language culture (e.g. marriage customs, food, educational system, etc.) followed by contrasting information from the students' native language culture.

③ Students prepare culture capsules for oral delivery during class.

④ Culture capsules may be done with the teacher giving a brief lecture on the chosen cultural point and then leading a discussion about the differences between cultures.

⑤ The teacher could also provide all of the information at once or could pause after the information in each paragraph and ask students about the contrasts they see.

(3) Culture Assimilators

Students listen to a description or watch an incident of cross-cultural interaction in which miscommunication occurs between a Korean and a member of the target culture. They choose from a list of alternatives an explanation of the episode and finally they read feedback paragraphs that explain whether each alternative is likely and why.

> ▶ Advantages of Culture Assimilator:
> - They are more fun to read.
> - They actively involve the student with a cross-cultural problem.
> - They have shown to be more effective in controlled experiments.
> - The content can be varied to suit the instructor's purpose.

(4) Cultural Minidramas

Students listen to, watch, or read a series of episodes in which miscommunication is taking place; each successive episode reveals additional information, with the exact problem in understanding revealed in the last part. Students are led in discussion in order to understand how misunderstandings arise when wrong conclusions are reached about the target culture on the basis of one's own cultural understanding.

(5) Culture Clusters

They consist of illustrated culture capsules, which develop a topic or related topics in a 30' classroom simulation, with the infomation contained in the capsule. The teacher acts as a narrator, guiding the skit through stage directions.

Culture and communication are inseparable because culture not only dictates who talks to whom, about what, and how the communication proceeds, it also helps to determine how people encode messages, the meanings they have for messages, and the conditions and circumstances under which various messages may or may not be sent, noticed, or interpreted... Culture... is the foundation of communication.

Culture capsules are one of the best-established and best-known methods for teaching culture. They have been tried mostly in classes for foreign language other than English. In conclusion, culture assimilators, culture capsules and culture clusters are techniques that represent a very simple and direct way of involving students in discovering other cultures.

📖 Further Reading ||||||||||||||||||||||||||||||||||||||||||||||||||||||||||||||||||||||||

Age & Acquisition

결정적 시기 가설(The Critical Period Hypothesis)에 따르면 인간이 언어를 학습함에 있어 보다 용이하게 습득할 수 있는 시기는 생물학적으로 결정되며, 이 시기가 지나면 언어 습득이 점점 어려워진다.

According to the Critical Period Hypothesis, animals including humans are genetically programmed to acquire certain kinds of knowledge and skill at specific times in life. Beyond those critical periods, it is either difficult or impossible to acquire those abilities. With regard to language, the CPH suggests that children who are not given access to language in infancy and early childhood will never acquire language if these deprivations go on for too long.

1. 신경학적 측면(Behaviorists' View): Hemispheric lateralization

사춘기 이전의 어린아이는 뇌의 유연성으로 인해 모국어뿐 아니라 제2언어를 습득할 수 있다. 그러나 사춘기 이후의 학습자는 뇌편중화가 완료되면서 좌뇌 위주의 학습을 하게 되므로 제2언어 학습에서 원어민과 같은 발음을 쉽게 습득하지 못하며, 언어 학습을 지나치게 분석적인 과업으로 수행한다.

The plasticity of the brain prior to puberty enables children to acquire not only their first language but also a second language and that possibly it is the very accomplishment of lateralization that makes it difficult for people to be able ever again to easily acquire fluent control of a second language, or at least to acquire it with what is called "authentic(nativelike)" pronunciation.

2. 인지적 측면(Cognitivists' View)

인간의 인지는 생후 16년 동안 급속도로 발달하며 성인이 된 후에는 그 속도가 줄어든다.

As the child matures into adulthood, the left hemisphere (which controls the analytical and intellectual functions) becomes more dominant than the right hemisphere (which controls the emotional functions). It is possible that the dominance of the left hemisphere contributes to a tendency to overanalyze and to be too intellectually centered on the task of second language learning.

> ▶ **평형화(Equilibration)**
>
> 인지는 불평형에서 평형으로 발달하는데, 형식적 조작기에 이르러서 평형 상태를 이룬다. 이때 인지적 불평형이 언어 습득의 동기를 제공한다.
>
> Conceptual development is a process of progressively moving from states of disequilibrium to equilibrium and that periods of disequilibrium mark virtually all

cognitive development up through age fourteen or fifteen, when formal operations finally are firmly organized and equilibrium is reached. It is conceivable that disequilibrium may provide significant motivation for language acquisition: language interacts with cognition to achieve equilibrium.

3. 정의적 측면(Constructivists' View)

언어 자아(language ego)란 특정 언어를 습득하는 과정에서 발달, 형성되는 자아 정체성을 가리킨다. 청소년 및 성인의 제2언어 학습 시 부딪칠 수 있는 어려움을 이 언어 자아로 설명할 수 있다. 사춘기 이전의 아동은 역동적이고 유동적인 자아를 가지고 있기 때문에 새로운 언어는 아동의 자아에 위협이나 억압이 되지 않는다. 그러나 학습자들은 사춘기 시기의 신체적·정서적·인지적 변화에 따라 자신의 자아를 방어하기 위한 방어기제인 억압(inhibition)을 형성하게 된다. 따라서 사춘기 이후에는 자신의 유약한 자아를 보호하기 위한 방어벽인 억압이 생성되므로 이 억압이라는 방어기제에 의해 청소년이나 성인들에게 있어서 새로운 언어를 학습한다는 것은 보다 어려운 일이 되는 것이다.

The language ego is the identity a person develops in reference to the language he or she speaks. It may account for the difficulties that adults have in learning a second language. The child's ego is dynamic and growing and flexible through the age of puberty. Thus a new language at this stage does not pose a substantial "threat" or inhibition to the ego. Then the simultaneous physical, emotional, and cognitive changes of puberty give rise to a defensive mechanism in which the language ego becomes protective and defensive. The language ego clings to the security of the native language to protect the fragile ego of the young adult.

4. 언어적 측면(Bilingualism, 언어적 처리 과정)

① **Coordinate bilinguals**: 제1언어와 제2언어의 언어 상황을 구별해 성공적인 두 언어 습득을 이루는데, 이때 아동은 두 개의 의미 체계를 구축하게 된다.

② **Compound bilinguals**: 제1언어를 습득한 후 제2언어를 학습하게 되는 성인은 하나의 의미 체계를 가지고 두 가지 언어를 사용한다.

③ **언어 학습의 방향**: 모국어와 목표 언어가 같은 환경 내에서 습득된 경우, 두 언어의 사용을 복합 이중 언어 사용(compound bilingualism)이라 하고, 모국어와 목표 언어가 별개의 환경에서 습득된 경우의 두 언어 사용을 병행 이중 언어 사용(coordinate bilingualism)이라 한다. 이 이론은 두 언어를 사용하되 각각 다른 환경이 어떻게 다른 의미 체계에 적용되는 지를 알아보기 위한 것이다. 예를 들면, 복합 이중어 사용자에게 'bread'는 '빵'이라는 한국어의 영어 번역에 불과하지만, 병행 이중어 사용자에게는 'bread'는 'bread'일 뿐이며, 또한 '빵'은 그저 '빵'일 뿐이다. 따라서 효과적인 외국어 학습을 위해 가능한 한 병행 이중 언어 사용자(coordinate bilinguals)로의 접근을 목표로 해야 한다.

Chapter
05

교수법

Chapter
05

교수법

---

1 Communicative Language Teaching

(1) Notional Functional Syllabus

① 언어 기능을 언어 습득의 구성 요소로 여기면서 기존의 구조주의 교수요목(structural syllabus)과 대조를 이룬다.

② 문법적 형태에 지나치게 집착했던 교수법에 반박하면서 언어 사용의 화용적 목적에 초점을 둔다.

③ **Notions**: 존재, 공간, 시간, 수량, 질 등의 추상적인 개념 및 감정을 표현하는 general notions와 문맥이나 상황에 따라 의미가 달라지는 specific notions로 이뤄진다.

④ **Functions**: reporting, suggesting, accepting, inviting, apologizing 등의 언어 기능으로 구성돼 있다.

(2) Communicative Competence

① **Grammatical Competence**: 언어의 음운적, 통사적, 의미적 체계에 대한 지식과 이러한 지식을 활용할 수 있는 능력이다.

② **Discourse Competence**: 문장 단위 이상인 담화의 유형 및 특징 등을 알고 적절하게 담화를 구성하거나 이해할 수 있는 능력으로, 글의 구성 능력(결합성, cohesion)과 표면적으로 관계가 없는 것처럼 보이는 발화의 의미 관계를 이해하는 일관성(coherence)에 관한 능력이다.

ⓐ **Cohesion의 실례**: 각 문장이 임의적으로 구성돼 있는 것이 아니라, 결합적 장치 (reference: Mr.Smith → he, a jewelry box → it / conjunction: however 등)에 의해 긴밀하게 구성돼 있다.

> **Ex** One day, Mr.Smith bought a jewelry box for his wife. After being home, *he* put *it* in the drawer. *However, he* forgot where *he* put *it*.

ⓑ **Coherence의 실례**: 표면적인 결합 장치가 보이지 않으나, 기능적인 측면에서 통일성을 보여주고 있다(A: 요구, B: 요구에 응할 수 없는 변명, C: 변명에 대한 수락).

> **Ex** A: This is a call for you.　　*(Request)*
> B: I'm in the bath.　　　　*(Excuse)*
> C: OK.　　　　　　　　*(Accept)*

③ **Socio-linguistic Competence**: 사회문화적 규칙과 담화 규칙에 대한 지식을 포함한다. 즉, 주어진 상황에 구두 및 문자 언어를 이해하고 적절하게 표현할 수 있는 능력을 말한다.

> **Ex** NS ：You are so lovely today!
> NNS：I'm shy. (→ Thank you.)
> ➡ 상황에 적절한 언어(칭찬 → 감사)를 사용하지 못한 에

④ **Strategic Competence**: 언어 지식의 부족으로 의사소통이 중단되려고 할 때 의사소통을 계속 이어가거나 의사소통의 효능을 향상시키기 위해 사용하는 의사소통 전략의 활용 능력을 말한다.

> **Ex** Operator ： This is a collect call from Sandra.
> Mother ： Sorry, she is not here!
> Operator ： *(adapting a child voice)* It's from Sandra.
> Mother ： Oh, I see. I'll get it!
> ➡ 의사소통의 문제가 발생하자 비언어적 수단을 사용해 의사소통의 단절을 해소한 예

• Models of Communicative Competence Compared •

Canale and Swain (1980)	1. Grammatical 2. Discourse 3. Sociolinguistic 4. Strategic

Bachman (1990)	Language Competence (with Strategic Competence as an "executive" function):
	A. Organizational competence
	    1. Grammatical
	    2. Textual (= Discourse)
	B. Pragmatic competence
	    3. Illocutionary (= Functions of language)
	    4. Sociolinguistic

Littlewood (2011)	1. Linguistic (= Grammatical) 2. Discourse (= Textual) 3. Pragmatic (= Strategic) 4. Sociolinguistic 5. Sociocultural

(3) Lesson Procedure

의사소통 언어 교수는 authentic materials를 사용해 학습자들에게 특정한 언어 기능 (predicting, persuading, suggesting, asking for directions, etc.)을 하나씩 제시하고 pair or group work에서 communicative activities(information-gap or role play, etc.)를 통해 의사소통 능력을 기르고자 한다.

Procedure	Notice
distributing a handout that is a copy of a sports column from a **recent newspaper**	whole class
telling the students to underline the reporter's **predictions**	individual work
giving the students the directions for the activity in the **target language**	teacher talk
letting students **unscramble** the sentences of the newspaper article	individual work

planning **language game** for students	group work
giving each group of students a strip and **a task** to perform	group work
planning a **role play** for students	group work
eliciting relevant vocabulary after doing role play	whole class work
giving a homework on listening to debate on the radio or watching it on television	homework

---

Plus ➕

General Approaches

1. Learner-centered Instruction

교사가 교실에서 모든 상황을 통제하는 교사 중심 수업(Teacher-centered Instruction)과는 달리 학습자 중심 수업(Learner-centered Instruction)은 학습자에 초점을 두고 수업 활동을 진행하는 것을 의미한다.

Being a learner-centered teacher means focusing attention squarely on the learning process: what the student is learning, how the student is learning, the conditions under which the student is learning whether the student is retaining and applying the learning, and how current learning positions the student for future learning. The distinction between teacher-centered and student-centered is made as a way of indicating that the spotlight has shifted from the teacher to the student. In learner-centered instruction the action focuses on what the students are doing not what the teacher is doing. This approach that now features students, accepts, cultivates and builds on the ultimate responsibility students have for their own learning. The idea of learner-centered instruction implies taking into account the learner's experiences, talents, personalities, social backgrounds, and needs. It also refers to using current knowledge about learning as a way to help learners become lifelong learners able to cope with the rapid changing world of their time.

05

2. Experiential and Project—based Learning

경험적인 언어 학습은 구체적인 경험을 통해 학습자들에게 실질적인 언어를 사용하도록 하는 Learning by Doing Approach의 일환으로 제시된다.

This educational framework starts from the context of the Communicative Language Teaching Movement and also is known as *Project—based Learning*. **Experiential learning** highlights giving students concrete experiences in which they must use language in order to fulfill the objectives of a lesson. Also, this educational concept emphasizes the psychomotor aspects of language is subsumed and reinforced. Through action, students are drawn into a utilization of multiple skills. Accordingly, its educational foundations lie in the advantages of "learning by doing," discovery learning, and inductive learning. As in the following example, it includes activities that contextualize language, integrate skills, and point towards authentic, and real—world purposes.

① Hands—on projects (e.g. publish a school newspaper)

② Field trips and other on—site visits (e.g. a recycling center or a fire station)

③ Research projects (e.g. the value of solar power)

④ Extra—class dinner groups (e.g. learning about Vietnamese cuisine)

⑤ Creating a video advertising a product (e.g. organic fruit)

As one of English Club activities, students decided to publish a school newspaper as Project Work.

Lesson Procedure

1st stage: class discussion

The students would work in their class, planning, in collaboration with the teacher, the content and scope of this project and specific language needs they might have. They might also devise some strategies for how they will carry out the tasks, such as assigning each other specific roles to fulfill.

2nd stage: carrying out each role

This stage typically takes place outside the classroom and involves the gathering of any necessary information. During the stage, students may well use all four skills in a natural, integrated fashion.

• conducting interviews & writing up their interviews

• taking photographs

• gathering printed or visual material

• laying out and printing and distributing the first edition of their newspaper

3rd stage and final stage: review and feedback from the teacher

Students review their project. They monitor their own work and receive feedback from the teacher on their performance.

---

3. Strategies-based Instruction

학습자들은 자신의 능력과 한계를 깨달았을 때 자신의 장점을 강화시키고 자신의 약점을 개선시켜 성공적인 언어 학습에 도달할 수 있게 된다. 따라서 자신이 선호하는 학습 스타일을 파악하고 전략적 기법을 토대로 필요한 학습 스타일과 전략을 키워 나가며 전략 기반 수업을 통해 extra-class assistance(self-help study guide)를 제공하도록 한다.

Building into your pedagogy ways for students to achieve this kind of strategic autonomy has come to be known as *strategies-based instruction*, also called learning strategy training as well as learner development/training. Among other characteristics, good language learners take charge of their own learning, seeking out opportunities to use the language, experiment with the L2, make guesses, use production tricks, allow errors to work for them, and learn from their mistakes. In order for learners to become self-driven independent learners beyond the classroom, they must be full aware of their own strengths, weaknesses, preferences, and styles, and be able to capitalize on that metacognition through the use of appropriate action in the form of strategic options.

4. Other Collaborative Approaches

의사소통 접근이 시작되면서 교실에서 학습자의 협력(collaboration)과 상호작용(interaction), 협동(cooperation) 등이 강조돼 왔다. 따라서, 이러한 특징은 교실 수업을 계획할 때 협력적 접근법(collaborative approaches) 등으로 이어지는데, 이는 구성주의(constructivism) 원리가 적용되는 것이다. 대표적인 구체적 학습 방법에는 *inquiry-based approach*가 있다.

Cooperative learning incorporated principles of learner-centered instruction encourages students to work together in pairs and groups since they share information and come to each other's aid. They are "team" whose players must work together in order to achieve goals successfully. Further any models that feature collaboration—in which students and teachers work together to pursue goals—promote communities of learners that cut across the usual hierarchies of students and teachers, necessitating a cautious approach in cultures with strong power distance norms between teachers and students.

Collaborative learning is a method of teaching and learning in which students team together to explore a significant question or create a meaningful project. A group of students discussing a lecture or students from different schools working together over the Internet on a shared assignment are both examples of collaborative learning.

Cooperative learning, which will be the primary focus of this workshop, is a specific kind of collaborative learning. In cooperative learning, students work together in small groups on a structured activity. They are individually accountable for their work, and the work of the group as a whole is also assessed. Cooperative groups work face-to-face and learn to work as a team.

In small groups, students can share strengths and also develop their weaker skills. They develop their interpersonal skills. They learn to deal with conflict. When cooperative groups are guided by clear objectives, students engage in numerous activities that improve their understanding of subjects explored.

Another example of a collaborative approach is found in **whole language education**, which emphasized the interconnections between spoken and written language.
① Language is not the sum of its many dissectible and discrete parts.
② Integrate the four skills (listening, speaking, reading, and writing).
③ Language is a system of social practices that both constrain and liberate.

5. Episode Hypothesis

에피소드 가설은 학습자에게 제공되는 학습 자료가 '이야기' 방식으로 제공될 경우 다른 유의미한 자료에 비해 더욱 효과적인 이해와 재생을 이끌어 낼 수 있다는 측면에서 의사소통 접근법에서 학습 자료의 제시 조건이 된다.

Text will be easier to reproduce, understand, and recall to the extent that is structured episodically.

또한, 이와 같은 에피소드 가설은 학습 상황에서 통합 수업 모형을 이끌어 낼 수 있다. 에피소드 가설에 근거를 둔 수업은 다음과 같다.
① Stories or episodes challenge the teacher and textbook writer to present interesting, natural language.
② Episodes can be presented in either written or spoken form.
③ Episodes can provide the stimulus for spoken or written questions that students respond to, in turn, by speaking or writing.
④ Students can be encouraged to write their own episodes, or to complete an episode whose resolution or climax is not presented.
⑤ Those written episodes might then be dramatized in the classroom by the students.

2 Task-Based Instruction

과제 기반 수업에서 학습자들은 언어의 형태에 초점을 두기 전에 수행해야 할 과제를 먼저 부여받고(deep-end strategy), 의미 협상 과정을 통해 과제를 완수해야 하며, 이 과정을 통해 언어 습득이 촉진된다.

(1) 과제 기반 수업의 학습 원리

① Meaning is primary through interaction in the target language.
② There is some communication problem to solve.
③ There is some sort of relationship to comparable real-world activities.
④ Task completion has some priority.
⑤ The assessment of the task is in terms of outcome.

Plus ➕

1. Task Type

	Interactant Relationship	Interaction Requirement	Goal Orientation	Outcome Options
Jigsaw	two-way	required	convergent	closed
Information Gap	one-way or two-way	required	convergent	closed
Problem Solving	one-way or two-way	optional	convergent	closed
Decision Making	one-way or two-way	optional	convergent	open
Opinion Exchange	one-way or two-way	optional	divergent	open

① Interactant Relationship

This concerns who holds the information to be exchanged and who requests it and supplies it in order to achieve the tasks.

② Interaction Requirement

This concerns whether the task requires participants to request and supply information or whether this is optional.

③ Goal Orientation

This concerns whether the task requires the participants to agree on a single outcome or allows them to disagree.

④ Outcome Options

This refers to the scope of the task outcomes available to the participants in meeting the task goals. In the case of 'closed' tasks a single outcome is required whereas 'open' tasks permit several possible outcomes.

2. 의사소통 활동으로서의 EFL 과제 유형: Communication Task (Prahbu)

① An Information-gap Activity

to involve the exchange of information among participants in order to complete a task.

② An Opinion-gap Activity

students give their personal preferences, feelings, or attitudes in order to complete a task.

③ A Reasoning-gap Activity

to derive some new information by inferring it from information they have been given.

➡ information-gap (single information transfer) / reasoning-gap / opinion-gap (too open-ended task) 중 더 효과적인 것은 보다 긴밀한 상호작용과 그룹 구성원 간의 활발한 정보 교류를 촉진하는 reasoning-gap task라고 할 수 있다.

(2) Task

① **Target task**: 학습자들이 교실을 벗어나 궁극적으로 완수해야 하는 실생활에서의
과제로, Notional-functional syllabus에서 제시됐던 언어 기능(function)과
유사하지만 목표 과제는 더 구체적이며 교실 수업과 보다 분명하게 관련이 있다.

> **Ex** Function: 개인 정보 제공하기
> Target task: 입사 면접시험에서 개인 정보 제공하기

② **Pedagogical task**: 수업 시간, 즉 교실 안에서 궁극적인 목표 과제 수행을 위해 의
도적으로 마련된 과제이다. 교육학적 과제(pedagogical task)를 많이 연습한 후에는
최종 교육학적 과제(climactic pedagogical task)를 통해 실제 목표 과제의 시뮬레이
션을 실시한다.

Classroom Procedure	Notice
• **Target task**: giving personal information in a job interview	giving a handout
• **Pedagogical tasks**	
– listening to extracts of authentic job interviews	whole class-listening comprehension
– drilling in the use of frequency adverbs	pair work
– exercising in comprehension of Wh-questions with do-insertion	
– analysing the grammar and discourse of the interviews	group work-discussion
– modeling an interview: teacher and student	presentation for the task
• **Climactic pedagogical task**	
– role–playing a simulated interview: students in pairs	pair work-role-play

(3) **Components of the TBL Framework** (Willis)

① **Pre-task**: introduction to topic and task

Teacher explores the topic with the class, highlights useful words and
phrases, helps students understand task instructions and prepare. Students
may hear a recording of other doing a similar task.

② Task cycle

    ⓐ **Task**: Students do the task, in pairs or small groups. Teacher monitors from a distance.

    ⓑ **Planning**: Students prepare to report to the whole class orally or in writing how they did the task what they decided or discovered.

    ⓒ **Report**: Some groups present their reports to the class or exchange written reports, and compare results.

③ Language focus

    ⓐ **Analysis**: Students examine and discuss specific features of the text or transcript of the recording.

    ⓑ **Practice**: Teacher conducts practice of new words, phrases and patterns occurring in the data, either during or after the analysis.

 기출 엿보기   2011학년도

Fighting Jet Lag

Pre-task

The teacher shows visual materials related to jet lag and elicits experiences from students.

Task Cycle 1

- The teacher asks students to brainstorm, in pairs, ways to overcome jet lag.
- Pairs select three items from what they have brainstormed.
- Pairs rehearse how to explain their choices and then present their list to the class with justifications.

Task Cycle 2

- The teacher distributes copies of a magazine article about overcoming jet lag and has students write down the three ways mentioned in the text.
- Pairs compare their list to that of the article.
- Students decide which pair has the most similar ways.

Post-task

- Students circle adverbial phrases expressing time and place in the magazine article.
- Students complete a grammar worksheet.

(4) PPP (Presentation-Practice-Production) Model & Task-based Instruction

When using the Presentation-Practice-Production teaching model a class is focused on a specific grammar structure presented by the teacher and practiced by the students in a controlled way during the practice stage but what it is noticeable is that during the production stage in which students are supposed to use the language freely, they simply ignore the structure they work on the previous stages and this could respond to the fact that we teachers might not prepare suitable activities which lead students to use such structure or students might use such structure some other day.

(5) Features of what happens in class when using each model

다음과 같이 language structure, students' and teachers' role, interaction and language exposure 측면에서 두 수업 모형의 차이점을 비교할 수 있다.

The PPP model	The task-based model
• The aim of a PPP lesson is to teach a specific language form—grammatical structure. • In a PPP cycle, with the presentation of the target language coming first, this context has to be created. • Students simply repeat, manipulate and apply the language. • In a PPP cycle, examples are made up to illustrate a single language item. • The teacher pre-selects the language to be taught. • A PPP cycle leads from accuracy to fluency. • PPP only provides a paradigm for grammar and form-focused lessons. • In a PPP lesson, except during the final production stage, teachers are at centre stage orchestrating the class. • Students are dependent.	• Learners use language from previous lessons. • Learners pay attention to specific features of language form at the end and when they reach the language focus, they are already familiar with it. • Students think and analyse. • Listening and reading provide more varied exposure to natural language. • Learners are free to ask about any aspects of language they notice. • A TBL cycle leads from fluency to accuracy. • All four skills are naturally integrated. • In TBL teachers intervenes only when needed. • Students are more independent. • Teacher works as a monitor.
presentation → practice → production	pre-task → task cycle → language focus

3 Content-Based Instruction

내용 기반 수업(content-based instruction)은 목표어(target language)와 내용(contents, subject) 학습을 통합하는 것으로, 주제 혹은 내용에 따라 언어 형태와 제시 순서를 결정하면서 언어 학습과 특정 내용 학습을 병행한다. 이때 언어가 학습자의 관심 분야의 내용을 전달하는 중간 매체 역할을 하기 때문에 학습자에게 내적 동기를 부여한다.

(1) Immersion Model

내용 기반 수업의 대표적인 형태인 몰입 수업(immersion model)은 내용교과를 목표어로 학습하기 때문에 언어의 4기능을 통합할 수 있으며, 학습자의 요구에 부합하는 학습이 가능하다. 목표어 학습을 위한 별도의 수업이 진행되지 않으며, 교사는 목표어와 해당 과목에 대한 지식을 지녀야 한다.

Immersion model is designed to teach both content and language simultaneously, based on the premise that people learn new languages in the course of learning other things. The features are as follows:

① It uses authentic materials or the same materials used by native speakers to learn the same content rather than materials specifically designed for language learners.

② The content instruction is tailored to the needs of the language learners.

③ The teachers have knowledge both about content and target language.

④ It has a natural integration of listening, speaking, reading and writing skills.

(2) Sheltered-language Instruction

In sheltered-language instruction, both native speakers and non-native speakers of a particular language follow a regular academic curriculum. For L2 students whose language proficiency is not quite able to handle subject-matter content in the L1 of the educational system, they provide opportunities for them to master content standards with added language assistance.

Sheltered-language instructors support their students through the use of particular instructional techniques and materials. It offers the significant advantage that second language students do not have to postpone their academic study until their language control reaches a high level. Pre-teaching difficult vocabulary, suggesting reading comprehension strategies, explaining certain grammatical structures, and offering form-focused feedback are among techniques that have shown to be helpful.

(3) Adjunct Model

In the adjunct model, students enroll in a regular academic course. Then, during the language class, the language teacher's focus is on helping students process the language in order to understand the academic content presented by the subject teacher. The language teacher also helps students to complete academic tasks.

(4) Theme-based Instruction(주제 중심 교수)

내용 기반 수업의 weak version으로, 해당 내용과 언어에 비슷한 비중을 둔다. 대표적인 학습 활동으로는 특정 주제에 대한 토론, 연구 프로젝트, 시뮬레이션 게임 등이 있다.

① 학습자의 관심사를 주제로 언어와 내용에서 다양한 흥미를 제공한다.

② 의미 있는 학습 상황에서 학습하려는 언어가 제공된다.

③ 학습자의 호기심과 학습 동기를 자극한다.

④ 4기능을 통합적으로 학습하고, 기능 간 습득을 촉진시킨다.

(5) Competency-based Instruction

Competency-based instruction, an effective form of content-based instruction for adult immigrants, offers students an opportunity to develop their second language skills at the same time that they are learning vital "life-coping" or "survival" skills such as filling out job applications or using the telephone.

In the Classroom

Competency: Returning an item to the store

1. Learners will be able to
- Explain reasons for returning an item.
- Demonstrate understanding of return policies: a refund, an exchange, or store credit.

2. Sample activity
Half of the class is assigned the role of store clerks. Each clerk is given store policies.

- Must have a receipt for a refund.
- Purchase made less than 30 days ago.
- Must have packaging for a refund.

Each of the other students in class is given an item to return.

3. Role-play
- Students return items to the appropriate store.
- Redistribute items and assign new clerk.

4. Follow-up
- Did you get a refund, a new item, or a store credit? Why? Did you get what you wanted?
- What were the store policies and how did they affect you?

02 \ Innovative Approach

1 Humanistic Approach

(1) Community Language Learning(집단 언어 학습, Non-defensive Learning)

① 수업 모형

> The students arrive and take their seats. The chairs are in a circle around a table that has a tape recorder on it. After greeting the students, the teacher introduces himself and has the students introduce themselves.
>
> In Korean, he tells the students what they will be doing that evening: They are going to have a conversation in English with his help. The conversation will be tape-recorded, and afterward, they will create a written form of the conversation—a transcript. He tells the class the rest of the evening will be spent doing various activities with the language on the transcript.

② 성공적인 학습의 조건: SARD

> security, attention, aggression, retention, reflection, discrimination

집단 언어 학습의 성공적인 수업을 위해서 학습자는 수업에서 안정감을 느끼고, 학습 내용에 주의 집중을 해야 하며, 자신이 배운 것을 과감하게 제시하고, 적극적으로 학습에 임해야 한다. 또한 학습한 내용을 효과적으로 보유하고 내재화하며, 자신의 학습 과정을 모니터링하고, 학습한 내용을 실제 교실 밖 의사소통 상황에서 적절하게 구별해 사용할 수 있어야 한다.

(2) Suggestopedia(암시 교수법)

암시 교수법은 물리적인 환경을 통해 학습자의 정의적인 여과막을 낮추고자 한다.

① 특징

ⓐ 학습의 주요 장애 요인을 학습에 대한 실패나 두려움 등의 심리적 장애로 보고 교사가 이를 제거해줌으로써, 학습자의 무한한 인지능력 및 무의식적인 자원을 이끌어 학습의 효율성을 달성하고자 하는 교수법이다.

ⓑ 주변적인 학습(peripheral learning): 학습 환경을 학습 효율성의 중요한 요소라 여긴다. 새로운 신분(new identity) 제공 및 학습의 성공에 대한 직·간접적인 암시를 통해 교실 지도가 이뤄진다.

② 수업 모형

> The teacher greets the students and explains that they are about to begin a new and exciting experience in language learning. She says confidently, *"You won't need to try to learn. It will just come naturally."* (성공적인 수업에 대한 직접적인 암시)
>
> First, you will all get to pick new names—English ones. "It will be fun," she says. Besides, she tells them they will need new identities (one they can play with) to go along with this new experience. She shows the class a poster with different English names printed in color. There are men's names in one column and women's names in another. She tells them that they are each to choose a name. She pronounces each name and has the students repeat the pronunciation.
>
> Next, she tells them that during the course they will create an imaginary biography about the life of their new identity. But for now, she says, they should just choose a profession to go with the new name. Using pantomime to help the students understand, the teacher acts out various occupations, such as pilot, singer, carpenter, and artist. The students choose what they want to be.

③ 시사점: The teacher should recognize that learners bring certain psychological barriers with them to the learning situation. She should attempt to desuggest these. Assuming a new identity enhances students' feeling of security and allows them to be more open. They feel less inhibited since their performance is really that of a different person.

(3) Silent Way(침묵 교수법, Production-based Approach)

Silent way에서는 교사가 침묵을 지키며, 학생들의 발견 학습을 통해 언어를 생성할 때 언어 습득이 촉진된다고 봤다.

① **Discovery learning**: 학습자를 학습의 주체로 보고 학습자 스스로 목표 언어의 규칙을 발견하도록 한다. 따라서 교사는 침묵으로 일관해 교실에서의 역할을 축소했다. 즉, 침묵 교수법은 학습자의 인지적 측면과 언어 생성을 보다 강조하고 있다.

ⓐ Learning is facilitated if learners discover and create rather than remember what is to be learned.

ⓑ Learning is facilitated by accompanying physical objects.

ⓒ Learning is facilitated by problem-solving including the materials to be learned.

② 특징

　ⓐ 음－색 도표(sound－color chart)를 짚어가며 기본 발음을 교수한다.

　ⓑ 발음에 어느 정도 익숙해지면 다양한 색깔의 길고 짧은 막대(rod)를 사용해서 의미를 지도한다.

　ⓒ 색상, 숫자, 'long, short' 등의 형용사와 'take, give, pick up, put, drop' 등의 동사로 시작해서 학생에게 행동하도록 지시한다.

　ⓓ 그림, 연습 문제, 스케치 등을 활용해서 광범위한 어휘를 다룬다.

③ 수업 모형

> The teacher walks to the front of the room, takes out metal pointer and points to a chart hanging above the blackboard. The blocks are arranged in rows. Each block is a different color. This is a sound-color chart. Each rectangle represents one English sound. There is a white horizontal line approximately halfway down the chart separating the upper rectangles, which represent vowel sounds, from those below the line, which represent consonant sounds. Without saying anything, the teacher points in succession to each of five blocks. Again, no one says anything. The third time, the teacher does the pointing, he says /a/ as he touches the first block. The teacher continues and taps the four other blocks of color with the pointer. As he does this, several students say /e/, /i/, /o/, /u/.

④ 장점

　ⓐ 시행착오를 통한 발견 학습을 강조함으로써 효과적으로 언어를 학습할 수 있다.

　ⓑ 학습자를 학습의 주체로 삼아 스스로 문제를 해결해 나가도록 한다.

⑤ 한계점

　ⓐ 교사가 의사소통적 분위기를 조성하게 되면 학생에게 지나치게 방관적으로 과도한 학습의 짐을 떠맡길 수 있다.

　ⓑ 교사의 도움으로 쉽고 명확하게 전달될 수 있는 내용을 알아가는 데 많은 시간을 허비하게 된다.

2 Comprehension-Based Approach

(1) Total Physical Response

전신 반응 교수법은 신체적으로 직접 반응하게 함으로써 언어를 배우도록 한다. 전형적인 TPR 수업은 교사의 명령문에 따라 학생들이 명령을 수행하는 것이다.

① 특징

   ⓐ It emphasizes listening and encourages a silent period.

   ⓑ Teacher gives commands in the target language, and students act out the commands.

② 수업 모형

> It is the first class of the year and the teacher introduces the method she will use to study English, "You will not speak at first. Rather, you will just listen to me and do as I do. I will give you a command to do something in English and you will do the actions along with me."
>
> In English the teacher says, "Stand up." As she says it, she stands up and she signals for the four volunteers to rise with her. They all stand up. "Sit down," she says and they all sit. Then, the teacher issues a new command, "Turn around." The students follow the teacher's example.
>
> As the last step of the lesson, the teacher writes the new commands on the blackboard. Each time she writes a command, she acts it out. The students copy the sentences from the blackboard into the notebooks.

Plus ➕

The Audio-Motor Unit

Audio-Motor Unit은 명령에 문맥적인 부분을 더함으로써 TPR의 명령과 동작들이 유의미한 연결이 이루어지지 않는다는 단점을 보완했다.

1. Features

① It includes a particular sequence of commands, all centering on a single topic.

> Ex | Topic: Set the table
>
> "Go to the cupboard, open the cupboard door, find the largest bowl, take it out, set it on the table."

② The teacher demonstrates the appropriate responses to the commands, using whatever realia are available to make the actions comprehensible.

③ The students are invited to comply with the commands.

④ It can include cultural learning in the lessons. Various customs involving eating, preparing food, telephone conversations, and introductions are taught through a series of commands given in the context of real or pretend situations.

2. Benefits

① The vocabulary, structures, and syntax of the language used in their lessons were reinforced by exposure to the audio-motor strategy.

② Students became strongly interested in the lessons through the physical acting out of cultural aspects.

③ The lessons, even though designed for the development of listening skills, had a real impact on oral production. The teachers noticed increased spontaneity and better pronunciation, although they admitted the latter was difficult to verify.

④ The nonnative teachers of the various languages felt that they improved their own skills with the languages they were teaching.

(2) The Natural Approach

Krashen의 Input Hypothesis를 주요 학습 원리로 삼는 교수법이다. 따라서 외국어 학습은 자연스러운 상황(communication)에서 다량의 언어적 입력으로 이뤄진다는 기본 원칙 하에 학습 초기 다량의 듣기 활동을 토대로 이해 능력 신장에 초점을 둔다.

① 수업 단계

ⓐ **Comprehension(pre-production)**: 이 단계에서 학생들은 침묵기(silent period)를 가지며 교사로부터 이해 가능한 언어 입력을 받아들인다.

- During this first stage, the students go through a silent period. They receive comprehensible input usually from the teachers. Often the total physical response is used.
- Simple responses to the comprehensible input may be made by gesturing, nodding, using the L1, answering "yes," or "no," giving names of people or objects as answers to questions.
- A lot of visuals, explanations, and repetitions are used.
- The teacher's speech is a little slower than usual. The intonation is reasonably normal except that key words receive a bit of extra emphasis.
- Students are not called upon to respond individually. Instead, questions are directed to the whole group, and one or several can respond.
- Key terms are written on the board, perhaps on the second or third time the students are exposed to them.

ⓑ **Early speech production**: 두 번째 단계에서 학생들은 점점 발화를 시작하면서 자신들의 중간언어를 발달시키고 정교화한다.

- The second stage generally begins with an extension of many activities used in the comprehension stage such as the sentence-completion response, in which a personalized question is asked and the answer is provided except for one word.
- Students gradually answer "Mike has dress" instead of just "Mike" to teacher's question "Who has on a blue dress?"
- The speech at first will contain many errors which should be dealt with only indirectly, for example, "Yes, Mike has on the dress," instead of "No, you should say, Mike has on the dress."

ⓒ **Speech emergence**: 학생들의 발화에 이미 변화가 시작됐기 때문에 두 번째 단계와 세 번째 단계를 나누는 것이 다소 모호하지만 이 단계에서는 학생들의 오류가 점점 줄어들며, 더 어렵고 도전적인 과제를 통해서 발화를 계속 확장해 나간다.

- The utterances become longer and more complex. Many errors are still made but, if enough comprehensible input has been internalized, they should gradually decrease as the students move toward full production.
- A large number of activities can be used that are somewhat more demanding and challenging but still within reach cognitively: music, poetry, role-playing, drama, affective activities, and problem-solving.
- Many of the activities can be extended to provide additional opportunities for development. For example, instead of simply answering questions about an application form, the students can now fill one out; instead of just following directions, they can begin to write their own sets of simple directions to see if others can follow them.

② 수업 모형

Lesson theme: Body Parts and Ailments
Student level: beginner level

Teaching Procedure 1

Step 1: Teacher displays visual of a person with body parts labeled. She begins by pointing to words and saying body parts (students repeat words only if comfortable with language).

Step 2: Teacher removes labels, distributes them, and has each learner affix label to correct body part.

Step 3: Teacher removes cards again. Students in class have a set of yes/no cards (yes one color, no another color). Teacher points to and says a body part, sometimes correctly and sometimes incorrectly. Learners hold up yes/no card according to whether the teacher said the right or wrong word.

Lesson theme: Washing a Car
Task type: problem solving
Student level: intermediate level

Teaching Procedure 2

Step 1: The teacher will guide the students in developing the vocabulary necessary to talk about the activity: rag, water, park, bucket, sponge, driveway

Step 2: Then together the class and instructor create utterances to describe the sequence of events to complete the activity. The class might say:
- *First I look for a bucket and a sponge or some rags.*
- *Then I park the car in the driveway.*
- *I use the hose to wash the car first with water only.*

These utterances are developed slowly with interspersed discussion.
- *Which is better to use, a sponge or a clean rag?*
- *Should you use soap or other cleaners (such as detergents) to wash a car?*

Step 3: After sequence is constructed, the discussion will broaden to include questions and discussion concerning the specific activity in the students' own lives.
- *How often do you wash your car? when? / where? / Do you enjoy it? / Why? / Why not?*

③ 한계점

ⓐ 침묵기와 관련해, 자연적 발화가 나타나지 않는 학습자와 서로 다른 시기에 자연적 발화를 보이는 학습자에 대한 설명이 불가능하다.

ⓑ '이해 가능한 입력'은 명시적으로 정의하기 어려운 개념이다.

ⓒ 언어 형태에 초점을 맞춘 명시적 교수의 부족으로 인해 오류 수정을 위한 직접적인 피드백이 전혀 없다.

(3) Lexical Approach & Concordance

① **Lexical Approach**: Lexical approach는 어휘(lexis)를 언어 학습의 가장 중요한 요소로 보고 개별 어휘 혹은 어휘의 덩어리(lexical chunks)를 학습의 기본 단위로 삼는다.

A lexical approach in language teaching is based on the belief that the building blocks of language learning and communication are not grammar, function, notions but lexis, that is, words and word combination.

Example ❶

S1 : I have to make an exam in the summer.
　　　(*T indicates mistake by facial expression.*)
S1 : I have to make an exam.
T　: (*Writes "exam" on the board.*)
　　　What verb do we usually use with "exam?"
S2 : Take.
T　: Yes, that's right. (*Writes "take" on the board.*)
　　　What other verbs do we use with "exam?"
S2 : Pass.
T　: Yes. And the opposite?
S1 : Fail.
　　　(*T writes "pass" and "fail" on the board.*)
T　: And if you fail an exam, sometimes you can do it again. What's the verb
　　　for that? (*Waits for response.*)
　　　No? OK, retake. You can retake an exam.
　　　(*Writes "retake" on the board.*)
　　　If you pass an exam with no problems, what can you say? I... passed.
S2 : Easily.
T　: Yes, or we often say "comfortably." I passed comfortably.
　　　What about if you get 51 and the pass mark is 50? What can you say? I...
　　　(*Waits for response.*)
　　　No? I just passed. You can also just fail.

Example ❷

Rearrange these to make fixed expressions with the verb (get).

1. Things much can't worse get.
2. What we to there are supposed time get?
3. I you the very weren't happy impression got.
4. We're we as as the for can far moment got.
5. We be to don't anywhere seem getting.
6. What you I can get?

Which of these suggests:

flying	offering	a drink	frustration	despair

② **Concordance**: 어휘 접근법의 대표적인 수업 모형으로 다량의 어휘 목록(corpora) 과 concordance program을 활용해 어휘를 직접적으로 지도한다. 주로 사용되는 collocation이나 문맥에 따른 어휘의 사용 등을 학습하는 데 효과적이다.

Example ❶

From Cobuild Direct Collocation, words collocated with "chocolate" (edited from top 100).

1. ◆ milk ◆	11. ◆ coffee
2. ◆ cake	12. plain ◆
3. hot ◆	13. ◆ fudge
4. white ◆	14. ◆ egg
5. ◆ cream	15. rich ◆
6. ◆ bar	16. box (of) ◆
7. dark ◆	17. eat ◆
8. ◆ mousse	18. ◆ biscuits
9. ◆ bars	19. ◆ ice
10. melted ◆	20. ◆ cocoa

Example ❷

is also a sign of trouble in	**paradise.**	9. maintaining love isn't
Grand Cayman is another diver's	**paradise,**	almost completely surrounded by
Socialist Republics-the workers	**paradise**	as it was once called earlier in
s garden, on the other hand, was a	**paradise**	at this time of year. Flowering
dormitory. It was a bachelor's	**paradise.**	Attractive, intelligent women
venerable past. Squaw is a skier's	**paradise**	because of the sheer variety and
South America, that he'd discovered	**paradise.**	Columbus also happened to think
Garden of Eden, but that image of	**paradise**	doesn't quite hold up in th 85
of Martha's Bineyard is known as a	**paradise**	for artists and photographers.
fee required to enjoy our shopper's	**paradise,**	home to world-famous Mrs. Knott's
intends to erect his gambler's	**paradise.**	I am not now, and nor have 1 ever
"paradise" is a cliche, but	**paradise**	it is. [p] Bitter End has 81
come over. I'm like-it was like	**paradise.**	It was just like, you know,
afforded; yet had we been even in	**paradise**	itself with these governors, it
into what they regard as the fool's	**paradise**	of interdisciplinary work. If the
The Apostles are a vacationer's	**paradise**	of sunshine, clear water, and deep
boutiques-a shopper's	**paradise**	that may even distract you from
war intruded even on this island	**paradise.**	The Coast Guard patrolled many of
stroll about this little slice of	**paradise,**	the animals seem to blend in with
techniques, this is a vision of a	**paradise**	to preserve, made in the USA in

03 \ Traditional Approach

1 Grammar Translation Method

(1) 특징

① It focuses primarily on reading and writing.

② It uses authentic texts.

③ Students have the same native language background.

④ It encourages students to translate rather than "think" in the target language.

⑤ It highlights grammar and vocabulary differences between the native and target languages.

⑥ Class is primarily conducted in the students' native language.

(2) 수업 모형

Exercise 1

These words are taken from the passage you have just read. Some of them are review words and others are new. Give the Korean translation for each of them. You may refer back to the reading passage.

ambition	gorgeous
career	loathe
wharf	envy
tranquil	humbly

Exercise 2

These words all have antonyms in the reading passage. Find the antonym for each:

| love | ugly |
| noisy | proudly |

---

(3) 한계점

① 듣기, 말하기를 철저히 무시하므로 의사소통 능력을 높이는 데는 거의 도움이 되지 않는다.

② 문자 중심의 번역과 문맥화되지 않은 어휘 암기의 비실용성, 예외를 강조하는 문법 규칙의 암기 등으로 학습자의 의욕을 저하시킨다.

③ 저자의 의도를 파악하는 진정한 읽기의 기능을 간과하고 있다.

2) Direct Method

문법 번역식 교수법(grammar−translation method)에 대한 반동으로 발달한 직접 교수법(direct method)은 문법 중심 교육과 번역을 지양하고 모국어 대신 목표어로 직접 가르치고자 한다.

(1) 수업 모형

The teacher is calling the class to order as we find seats toward the back of the room. He has placed a big map of the United States in the front of the classroom. He asks the students to open their books to a certain page number. The lesson is entitled "Looking at a Map." As the students are called on one by one, they read a sentence from the reading passage at the beginning of the lesson. The teacher points to the part of the map the sentence describes after each has read his sentence.

Lesson Theme: Looking at a Map

Exercise 1

Students read a sentence out loud and supply the missing word as they are reading.

• The Atlantic Ocean is _____ the East Coast.
• The Rio Grande is _____ Mexico and the United States.
• Edordo is looking _____ the map.

Exercise 2

• Review the features of United States geography.
• Following the teacher's directions, label blank maps with these geographical features. After this, the students will give directions to the teacher, who will complete a map on the blackboard.
• Practice the pronunciation of "river" paying particular attention to the /I/ in the first syllable (and contrasting it with /iy/) and to the pronunciation of /r/.

(2) 한계점

① 모국어 사용을 완전히 배제함으로써 설명할 때 시간이 낭비될 수 있다.

② 미숙한 학생들은 구문을 정확히 추론하기 어렵다.

③ 추상적인 내용을 명확히 전달하기 어렵다.

④ 원어민 수준의 외국어 구사 능력을 갖고 있는 고도로 훈련된 교사를 찾기가 어렵다.

3 Audiolingual Method

행동주의 학습 이론을 바탕으로 목표어를 올바른 형태로 반복 연습하고 지속적인 긍정적 강화를 함으로써 학습자들에게 목표어 학습이라는 좋은 습관(habit formation)을 심어주고자 한다.

(1) 특징

① It emphasizes listening and speaking.

② It focuses on oral language as it is used by native speakers.

③ It sequences grammar according to similarities and differences with the native language (contrastive analysis).

④ It uses memorized dialogues and pattern drills.

⑤ It encourages students to internalize language patterns within little or no grammatical explanation.

⑥ It requires well-pronounced, grammatically correct, full-sentence responses from students.

(2) 수업 모형

As we enter the classroom, the first thing we notice is that the students are attentively listening as the teacher is presenting a new dialog, a conversation between two people. The students know they will be expected to eventually memorize the dialog the teacher is introducing. All of the teacher's instructions are in English. "All right, class, I am going to repeat the dialog now."

Sally : Good morning, Bill.
Bill　: Good morning, Sally.
Sally : How are you?
Bill　: Fine, thanks, And you?
Sally : Fine, Where are you going?
Bill　: I'm going to the post office.
Sally : I am too, Shall we go together?
Bill　: Sure, Let's go.

"Listen one more time. This time try to understand all that I am saying." Now, the teacher has the whole class repeat each of the lines several times before moving on to the next line. When the class comes to the line, "going to the post office," they stumble a bit in their repetition. The teacher, at this point, stops the repetition and uses a backward build-up drill. Little by little the teacher builds up the phrases until the entire sentence is being repeated.

T　: Repeat after me: post office.
Ss : Post office.
T　: To the post office.
Ss : To the post office.
T　: Going to the post office.
Ss : Going to the post office.
T　: I'm going to the post office.
Ss : I'm going to the post office.

Through this step-by-step procedure, the teacher is able to give the students help in producing the troublesome line. Having worked on the line in small pieces, the students are also able to take note of where each word or phrase begins and ends in the sentence.

(3) 한계점

① 문형 연습과 단순한 모방 및 암기를 통한 학습은 학습자가 내용을 전체적으로 이해하지 못한 채 단기 기억에 머물기 때문에 실제 대화 상황에서 언어능력으로 전이되지 못한다.

② 기계적인 반복 훈련과 과도한 학습(over learning)은 학습자의 흥미를 잃게 한다.

Memo

Chapter
06

교재 개발 및 교재 분석

Chapter 06 교재 개발 및 교재 분석

01 Authentic Materials

1 Definition

*Authentic materials*는 목표 문화권의 화자에 의해 생성된 담화 및 글을 의미하는 것으로, 현재 진행되는 외국어 교실 수업에서 학습 자료로 선택해야 할 것인지에 대한 찬반이 엇갈리고 있다. 따라서 교사는 학습 자료로 authentic material을 선택할 경우 장단점을 명확하게 파악하고 학습자의 수준을 고려한 다음, 어떻게 authentic material을 교실 수업에서 제시해야 할 것인지 생각해야 한다.

There are number of definitions related to authentic materials; ① an authentic text is a stretch of oral language, produced by a real speaker or writer for a real audience and designed to convey a real message of some sort ② authentic texts (either written or spoken) are those which are designed for native speakers; they are text designed not for language students, but for the speakers of the language in question, and ③ a rule of thumb for authentic specially produced for propose of language teaching.

In the Classroom

Role Play

Situation 1: An evening's viewing

Work in pairs or groups of three.

You want to watch television tonight.
Look through the following Programme Guide and try to decide which programme to watch.
One person starts: '*What shall we watch tonight?*'

TV/RADIO | Programme guide by Celia Brayfield

BBC 1

12.35.—On the Move. 12.45.—Midday News. 1.0.—Pebble Mill. 1.45.—Trumpton. 2.0.—You and Me. 2.35.—For Schools, Colleges. 3.0.—Children's Wardrobe. 3.55.—Play School. 4.20.—Winsome Witch. 4.25.—Jackanory. 4.40.—Scooby Doo. 5.0.—John Craven's Newsround. 5.5.—Blue Peter. 5.35.—Paddington. 5.40.—Evening News. 5.55.—Nationwide. 6.45.—Tomorrow's World.

7.10 TOP OF THE POPS with Earth, Wind and Fire, ELO, Blondie, Real Thing, The Stranglers, Manhattan Transfer and Abba.

7.40 THE GOOD LIFE : Just My Bill. The rates bill sends farmer Briers off to market to sell his compost-grown wholefood. Also starring Felicity Kendal and Penelope Keith.

8.10 WINGS: Officer and Gentlemen. Young Farmer (Tim Woodward), with promotion on his mind, accidentally shoots down a peaceful German. More of the World War I flying aces.

9.0 NEWS with Angela Rippon, Weather.

9.25 CANNON : Bloodlines. Grieving father hires overweight detective to investigate doubtful suicide of brilliant son. Starring William Conrad.

10.15 OMNIBUS : Warsaw Autumn. A film by Dennis Marks, whose work can be expected to be confident, intelligent and in keeping with the sombre beauties of Northern Europe's artistic capitals, about last year's modern music festival in Warsaw. The film reports on the reflowing of the arts in Poland, and the meeting of the country's two leading resident composers, Lutoslawski and Penderecki, with her most notable musical exile, Andrzej Panufnik.

11.0 TONIGHT investigates top people's crime wave — highly organised trade in stolen Rolls-Royces. 11.40.—Weather.

BBC 2

7.0 NEWS, Weather. 7.5.—**Your Move** with Brian Redhead, Terence Alexander, Fenella Fielding and Julian Holloway. (Repeat.)

7.30 NEWSDAY with Michael Charlton and Richard Kershaw.

8.10 LIVING IN THE PAST : March. The start of an intriguing report on an experiment in Iron Age living. Six young couples and three children have been living in secret in the West Country under the farming methods and the survival secrets of Iron Age tribesmen. They have planted prehistoric strains of wheat, herded ancient breeds of sheep and goats, out what needed to be cut with stone axes and lived in primitive shelters. This opening programme shows how the group was chosen, trained and installed in an ancient British settlement.

9.0 GARDENERS' WORLD. Back in the days of bio-humus and Gro-bags, blind gardener Bob Roberts joins Peter Seabrook and Arthur Billitt on the modern farm.

9.25 JEREMIAH JOHNSON. (1972) (A). Robert Redford, Will Geer. Scenic if slightly worthy story of an idealistic ex-soldier taking to the hills of Utah to live at one with nature. Nature is less hospitable than expected, and the advice of a veteran trapper is all that saves our hero from the mountain winter.

11.10 NEWS, Weather. 11.20.—**Men of Ideas:** Logical Positivism and its Legacy. Sir Alfred Ayer joins Bryan Magee in this heavyweight series on leading Western philosophers. 12.0.—Music At Night.

ITV ANGLIA, as London except :
1.25.—Anglia News. 2.0.—Women Only. 4.20.—The Secret Lives of Waldo Kitty. 4.45.—Solo One. 5.15.—Emmerdale Farm. 6.0.—About Anglia. 6.20.—Arena. 7.0.—Bygones. 7.30.—Now Who Do You Do? 10.30.—Polk in the East. 11.0.—Film: The Mystery of the Wax Museum. 12.30.—The Living Word.

ITV

12.0.—Charlie's Climbing Tree. 12.10.—Stepping Stones. 12.30.—Make It Count. 1.0.—News. 1.20.—Help! 1.30.—Crown Court. 2.0.—After Noon. 2.25.—Shades of Greene. 3.20.—Quick on the Draw. 3.50.—The Sullivans. 4.20.—Little House on the Prairie. 5.15.—Mr and Mrs. 5.45.—News. 6.0.—Thames at 6. 6.35.—Crossroads.

7.0 THE BIONIC WOMAN : The Night Demon. Return of the slow motion Amazon (Lindsay Wagner) who unwisely visits the teepee of an Indian mythology buff.

8.0 ROBIN'S NEST : As Long As He Needs Me. Return of this amiable comedy series set in a bistro run by Richard O'Sullivan.

8.30 ARMCHAIR THRILLER : Rachel In Danger. Second instalment of this new thriller series, in which 11-year-old swot Rachel discovers the body in the cupboard, and the plotting terrorists fall out.

9.0 GEORGE AND MILDRED : Your Money or Your Life. Battling marrieds squabble over insurance. With Yootha Joyce and Brian Murphy. (Repeat.)

9.30 THIS WEEK : Jonathan Dimbleby reports from Ethiopia, now fighting three wars.

10.0 NEWS.

10.30 TIME FOR BUSINESS brought New York women's rights campaigner Gloria Greenberg over to discuss the Equal Pay Act with Barbara Castle. 11.15.—Kitchen Garden: Buyez British! Keith Fordyce and Claire Rayner on planting your own vineyard. 11.45.—What the Papers Say with Peter Paterson. 12.0.—Close.

ITV SOUTHERN, as London except :
1.20.—Southern News. 2.0.—Women Only. 4.20.—Betty Boop. 4.25.—Little House on the Prairie. 5.20.—Crossroads. 6.0.—Day by Day. 6.30.—University Challenge. 7.0.—Emmerdale Farm. 7.30.—Hawaii Five-O. 10.30.—Westside Medical. 11.30.—Southern News Extra. 11.40.—What the Papers Say. 12.0. — Weather; Children, Books and God.

Situation 2: Choosing a day tour

Work in pairs or groups of three.

You are staying in Eastbourne and want to go somewhere for the day. Look through the following Tour Guide and try to find somewhere to go. One person starts: *'What do you fancy doing today?'*

COACHDAY Eastbourne Area

Hampton Court Palace

This magnificent Palace on the banks of the River Thames was built by Wolsey and presented to King Henry VIII in 1526. At the rear, large additions were made by Wren for King William III, including the attractive Fountain Court. Of particular interest are also the Great Kitchen, the Great Vine and the Wine Cellars, the Maze and the Flower Gardens.

Depart 1000 Return 2000 Fare £ 2.25

Canterbury

This ancient city whose history can be traced to Roman and Medieval times in dominated by the Cathedral, the building of which was started in the 12th century and continued until the early 15th century, Thoman à Becket was murdered in the Cathedral in 1170 and from that date until King henry VIII destroyed the Martyr's Shrine it was a place of pilgrimage from all over Europe. The Norman Crypt is the largest in the world.

Depart 0930 Return 1730 Fare £ 1.65

2 Criteria for Selecting Authentic Materials

(1) Interest

진정성 있는 자료를 선택하는 데 있어서 그 자료의 주제가 가르치는 학생들의 요구 및 관심과 연관돼야 한다.

Authentic materials are taken from real life and are going to be introduced in the artificiality of the classroom. So a teacher has to ensure that the topic of the authentic materials chosen addresses the needs and interest of the specific group of students being taught.

(2) Purpose of Language Learning

자료를 선택하는 데 있어서 학생들이 영어 학습을 하는 목적이 고려돼야 한다.

The goal of language learning for that particular group of learners should be kept in mind while deciding which materials to use in class. The utility value of the materials is a very important consideration. The teacher has to consider if the information included in the materials chosen is of value to the students.

(3) Cultural Appropriateness

모국어의 문화와 상이한 문화적 배경을 지닌 자료를 선택할 경우, 학생들에게 그 배경을 설명하는 데 시간을 할애해야 하므로 본 과업에 할당할 시간이 줄어들 수 있다. 따라서 진정성 있는 자료를 선택함에 있어서 문화적 적절성이 고려돼야 한다.

Some of the materials are based on the native speaker's culture and for some learners it may be quite alien. Then the problem of explaining the culture to the students takes up a lot of class time and less time is devoted to the actual task based on the authentic material. Hence a teacher has to consider, whether the students have the background knowledge or cultural schema for the topic, while selecting materials.

(4) Language Level

진정성 있는 자료는 학생들의 언어적 수준을 고려해서 선택돼야 한다. 단 언어적 입력은 학생들이 이해할 수 있되, 그들의 동기를 유지할 수 있을 정도로 충분히 도전적이어야 한다.

While choosing the materials the most important factor is the level of the language used in the materials. These materials are taken from real life and not manipulated for the specific purpose of teaching a language in a classroom. The input has to be comprehensible to the students. At the same time the input should be challenging enough to sustain their motivation. If it is too below their level, they may not learn much from it, and if it is too above their level they will not be able to understand and interact with the materials.

	Important Factors in Choosing Authentic Reading Material
Suitability of Content	• Does the text interest the student? • Is it relevant to the student's needs? • Does it represent the type of material that the student will use outside of the classroom?
Exploitability	• Can the text be exploited for teaching purposes? • For what purposes should the text be exploited? • What skills/strategies can be developed by exploiting the text?
Readability	• Is the text too easy/difficult for the student? • Is it structurally too demanding/complex? • How much new vocabulary does it contain? Is it relevant?
Presentation	• Does it "look" authentic? • Is it "attractive?" • Does it grab the student's attention? • Does it make him want to read more?

3 Benefits, Drawbacks and Alternatives

(1) Benefits

텍스트가 지닌 진정성으로 인해 실제 생활에서 쓰이는 언어를 경험하고 학습할 수 있으며, 특히 목표 문화 학습에도 유용하다.

Through exploring these materials, students have the opportunity to see and hear real language that serves a purpose. Another convincing reason to use authentic samples is for their richness in cultural content. Because these texts are prepared for native speakers, they reflect the details of everyday life in a culture as well as its social value.

(2) Drawbacks

진정성 있는 텍스트는 일반적으로 학생들의 수준을 고려하지 않은 있는 그대로의 자료이기 때문에 학생들의 동기를 감소시키거나 학습의 효과를 떨어뜨릴 수 있다.

One of the challenges teachers often describe when using authentic texts is that these materials contain linguistic structures and vocabulary that students may not have already learned. Also, text is simply text, with varying levels of sophistication or complexity, which can demotivate students.

06

Plus ➕

Authentic Reading Materials

Advantages	Disadvantages
• "Real" language exposure with language change/variation reflected. • Students are informed about what is happening in the world. • Textbooks tend not to include incidental/improper English and become outdated very quickly. • The same piece of material can be used for different tasks. • Ideal for teaching/practising mini-skills-skimming/scanning. • Contain a wide variety of text types, language styles not easily found in conventional teaching materials. • Encourage reading for pleasure, likely to contain topics of interest.	• Often too culturally biased, difficult to understand outside the language community. • Vocabulary might not be relevant to the student's immediate needs. • Too many structures are mixed so lower levels have problems decoding the texts. • Special preparation is necessary, can be time consuming. • Can become outdated easily, e.g. news stories, articles.

(3) Alternatives

진정성 있는 텍스트의 단점을 보완하는 방법으로는 ① 학생들의 수준을 고려해서 제작된 교재를 사용하거나, ② 텍스트의 진정성은 살리되 어휘나 문장 구조를 단순화하거나 (simplifying), ③ 학생들에게 제공되는 과업의 수준을 조절하는 방법이 있다.

① Teachers can use the teacher-prepared textbook or commercial textbook.

② **Text simplification**: Simplifying the vocabulary and structure in the textbook while authenticity is not damaged.

③ **Task simplification**: Instead of simplifying the language of text, simplify the task that is demanded to the students.

02 \ Syllabus

1 Structural Syllabus

This type of syllabus contains *a collection of the forms* and *structures*, usually *grammatical of the language*. It covers nouns, verbs, adjectives, statements, questions, complex sentences, subordinate clauses, past tense and other aspects of language form such as pronunciation or morphology. Structural syllabi have most been associated with Grammar Translation Method, Audiolingualism, Silent Way.

2 Notional-Functional Syllabus

This type of syllabus contains *a collection of the functions* that are performed when language is used. It includes *informing, agreeing, apologizing, requesting, promising*, and so on. Examples of notions include size, age, color, comparison, time, etc.

06

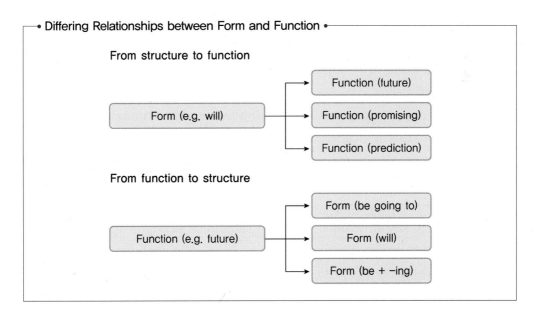

• Differing Relationships between Form and Function •

From structure to function

Form (e.g. will) → Function (future)
Form (e.g. will) → Function (promising)
Form (e.g. will) → Function (prediction)

From function to structure

Function (e.g. future) → Form (be going to)
Function (e.g. future) → Form (will)
Function (e.g. future) → Form (be + -ing)

Ex Introduce self [function] to other people [notion]

Ask for information [function] at a bank [notion]

Give directions [function]

Read the text [function] and answer [function] the questions [notion]

From the examples, it is clear that you can have function with a notion, a function alone, or several functions with a notion.

3 Situational Syllabus

A situational syllabus contains *a collection of real or imaginary situations* in which language occurs or is used. It usually involves several participants who are engaged in some activities in a specific setting. The primary purpose is to teach the language that occurs in the situations. For examples: *Seeing the dentist, buying a book at the book store, meeting a new student, asking directions in a new town, etc.*

The situational syllabus is closely related to the **topical syllabus**. The situational model will comprise units indicating specific situations, such as 'At the Post Office,' 'Buying an Airline Ticket,' or 'The Job Interview.' The topical or thematic syllabus is similar, but generally employs the procedure of grouping modules or lessons around a topic, something like barnacles clinging to the hull of a ship.

In this approach, the use of dialogues is very common as these form the basis of communication within a specific situation. However, the use of dialogues in the situational syllabus is quite different from the use of dialogues in a structural syllabus such as the Audiolingual Method. In the Audiolingual Method, specific structured dialogues are drilled and memorized and used to conceptualize key structures, while the situational dialogue approach is "aimed at meaningful conversational interchange in specific contexts." This means that the dialogues used in the situational syllabus, don't have language structures as their main focus, but rather their communicative effectiveness within a given situation.

4 Task-Based Syllabus

This type of syllabus is similar with content-based syllabus. Both of these syllabus do not organize the teaching with the linguistics features of the language being learned. It contains *a series of complex and purposeful tasks* that the students want or need to perform with the language they are learning.

5 Product-Oriented Syllabus and Process-Oriented Syllabus

A product-oriented syllabus focuses on things learned at the end of the learning process (outcomes) while **a process-oriented syllabus** focuses on the skills and processes involved in learning language. Thus, process-oriented syllabi are developed as a result of a sense of failure in product-oriented syllabi to enhance communicative language skills.

Plus ➕

Product-oriented Syllabus vs. Process-oriented Syllabus

Case 1
Students work with grammatical structures in their English course and they will show their progress at the end of the term by answering a grammar test.

Case 2
A writing lesson would focus on the processes writers use to complete their tasks, such as collecting information, organizing ideas, drafting and revising, rather than just the features of the products of writing, such as letters, compositions, notes, reports etc.

---

(1) Product-oriented Syllabi

Ex   ① Structural syllabus
② Situational syllabus
③ Notional/Functional syllabus

(2) Process-oriented Syllabi

Ex   ① Procedural/Task-based syllabus
② Learner-centered syllabus
③ Content syllabus

03 \ Textbook Adaptation

교사나 교과 전문가에 의해 만들어진 텍스트를 학습자에게 보다 적합한 자료로 만들기 위해서는 다음과 같은 방법들이 있다.

Adapting and supplementing the texts we choose can bridge the gaps that exist between a textbook and learner needs. This can be achieved by adding visuals, realia, and authentic materials, by adjusting activities to promote more interaction, or by implementing activities in ways that appeal to multiple intelligences and learning styles.

1 Adding

기존의 텍스트에 양 혹은 질적으로 자료를 추가함으로써 텍스트를 보완한다.

Materials are supplemented by putting more into them. The teacher can do this by either extending or expanding.

(1) Extending

같은 학습 내용이나 같은 수준의 연습 활동 등을 추가하는 등 양적으로만 자료를 추가하는 방법이다.

The teacher supplies more of the same type of material, thus making a quantitative change in the material. This means that the techniques are being applied within the methodological framework of the original materials.

Ex❶ There is a practice which asks the learner to complete a sentence with the missing verb in the correct form, such as the simple past. The coursebook may have provided ten sentences for this treatment, but the teacher may value this type of activity for her class and adapt the coursebook by adding five more sentences with missing verbs.

Ex❷ The materials contain a practice in the pronunciation of minimal pairs (rice/lice, rake/lake) but not enough examples of the difficulties for learners with a particular L1. Thus, the teacher put more examples with /r/, /l/ minimal pairs.

(2) Expanding

기존의 자료와는 다른 기능을 다룬 연습 활동이나 다른 차원의 언어 접근법을 적용한 연습 활동을 추가하는 등 텍스트를 질적으로 추가하는 것을 의미한다.

Expanding adds something different to the materials; the change is qualitative. The expanding goes further than extending by putting in a different language skill or a new component.

> **Ex❶** The only pronunciation practice in the materials is on individual sounds and minimal pairs, however, this may be necessary but not sufficient. Therefore, the teacher decides to add some work on sentence stress.

> **Ex❷** Although the new grammar material is important and relevant, the addition of a discussion section at the end of the unit will help to reinforce and contextualize the linguistic items covered.

(2) Deleting

기존 텍스트에서 불필요한 부분을 생략하는 것으로, Adding과 마찬가지로 양적인 방법과 질적인 방법이 있다.

Deletion is the opposite process to that of addition by omitting materials from the original.

(1) Subtracting

동일한 언어 기능 내에서 지나치게 많은 연습 활동을 생략하는 등 양적으로 텍스트를 줄이는 것을 의미한다.

Subtracting refers to reducing the length of materials in quantitative way. It does not have a significant impact on the overall methodology.

> **Ex** A teacher decides to do five of the questions practising the simple past tense instead of the ten in the coursebook.

(2) Abridging

여러 기능을 다룬 연습 활동 중 질적으로 다르고 불필요한 활동을 생략하는 것을 말한다.

Abridging means omitting materials qualitatively, making the changes greater than subtracting.

> **Ex❶** The material contains a discussion section at the end of each unit. However, our learners are not really proficient enough to tackle this adequately. Thus, the teacher may delete this kind of training.

> **Ex❷** Students on a short course are working with communicative materials because of their instrumental reasons such as international business trip or visit as tourists. The lengthy grammatical explanations accompanying each functional unit are therefore felt to be inappropriate.

3 Modifying

학습자의 요구나 언어 접근법에 맞춰 적절하게 텍스트의 내용이나 수업의 형식적인 면을 수정하는 것을 말한다.

Modifying refers to a change in the nature or focus of an exercise, or text, or classroom activity. Currently the most frequently stated requirement for a change is for materials to be made more communicative. Therefore, modifying may relate activities more closely to learners' own backgrounds and interests, introducing models of authentic language.

(1) Rewriting

학습자의 요구나 특정 교수법(특히 CLT)에 맞춰 텍스트의 내용을 수정하는 기법을 말한다.

Rewriting means an internal change that can be applied to any aspect of content.

> **Ex❶** Some of end-of-text comprehension questions are more like a test, where students can answer by "lifting" the information straight from the text. These questions can be modified so that students have to interpret what they have read or heard.

Ex❷ A story about an English family, with English names, living in an English town, eating English food and enjoying English hobbies can in fact be modified quite easily by making a number of straightforward surface changes.

(2) Restructuring

학습 상황에 보다 적합하게 학생들의 활동이나 교실(혹은 그룹) 배치를 조정하는 방법을 말한다.

Restructuring can be applied to classroom management.

Ex❶ The materials may contain role-play activities for groups of a certain size. It will probably be necessary to assign one role to a number of pupils at the same time. Obviously the converse—here the class is too small for the total number of roles available—is also possible.

Ex❷ A written language explanation designed to be read and studied can be made more meaningfully if it is turned into an interactive exercise where all students participate.

4 Simplifying

학습자들의 이해를 높이기 위해 단어, 문법, 문장 길이 등 언어의 수준을 조절하는 방법을 말한다.

When simplifying, the teacher could be rewording instructions or text in order to make them more accessible to learners, or simplifying a complete activity to make it more manageable for learners and teachers. There is a distinct danger of distorting language when attempting to simplify a text and thus making the text inauthentic.

(1) Sentence Structure

Sentence length is reduced or a complex sentence is rewritten as a number of simpler ones, for example, by the replacement of relative pronouns by nouns and pronouns followed by a main verb.

(2) Lexical Content

The number of new vocabulary item is controlled by reference to what students have already learned.

(3) Grammatical Structure

For example, passives are converted to actives; simple past tense to simple present; reported into direct speech.

5 Reordering

연습 활동이나 자료 제시를 교육적인 관점에서 보다 더 적합한 순서로 변경하는 방법을 말한다.

The teacher makes materials more pedagogically sensible by sequencing activities in a different order.

Ex❶ Materials typically present "the future" by "will" and "going to." However, for many students, it is helpful to show the relationship between time reference and grammatical tense in a more accurate way. The teacher would include the simple present and the present continuous as part of the notion of "futurity" using "Next term begins on 9 September" as illustrations.

Ex❷ The teacher can begin with a general discussion before looking at a reading passage rather than using the reading as a basis for discussion.

04 \ Material Evaluation

1 External Evaluation

자료의 목차나 표지에 나와 있는 객관적인 사실을 바탕으로 교재를 분석하는 방법으로, analysis level 1이 해당된다.

(1) External evaluation is concerned to obtain a general impression of the material; wide-ranging but relatively superficial.

(2) the impressionistic method

(3) This overview typically involves glancing and skimming through the book such as:

① the blurb, or the claim made on the cover of the teacher's or students' book
② the introduction and table of contents

2 Internal Evaluation

표면적으로 드러난 사실 이외에 자료가 담고 있는 의미까지 분석하는 것으로, analysis level 2와 3이 이에 가깝다고 볼 수 있다.

(1) In-depth techniques go beneath the publisher's and author's claims to look at.

(2) the in-depth method

• Analysis Level •

Level	Focus of Analysis	Examples of features to be considered
1	What is there	publication date, intended users, type of material, classroom time required, intended context of use, physical aspects (durability, components, use of colour), the way the materials is divided up across components, how the student's book is organized, how learners and teachers are helped to find their way around
2	What is required of users	**Tasks** • what the learner has to do • whether their focus will be on form, meaning or both • what cognitive operations will be required • what form of classroom organization will be involved (e.g. individual work, whole class) • what medium will be involved • who will be the source of language or information
3	What is implied	selection and sequencing of content (syllabus) and tasks, distribution of information across teacher and student components, reconsideration of information collected at levels 1 and 2

05 \ Computer-Assisted Language Learning

1 Corpus Linguistics in the Classroom

교사와 학습자는 교실에서 다양한 방법으로 코퍼스를 활용할 수 있다. 가령, 교사는 학생들의 과제물을 모아 콘코던스 프로그램을 이용해 전형적인 오류 패턴을 조사할 수 있는데, 이때 학생들의 글쓰기에서 나타난 오류들은 교재 개발의 기초 자료가 된다. 또한 교사는 원어민의 글들에 대한 코포라를 통해 학생들에게 예시 문장을 제시하고 연습하게 할 수 있으며, 학습자들도 콘코던스나 코포라 프로그램을 배워서 'look'과 'see'의 차이를 찾는 등 문법 구조, 숙어와 용례 등을 찾을 때 스스로 활용할 수 있다(Data Driven Learning).

Both teachers and learners can use corpus linguistics in various ways within the classroom. A teacher might collect a set of student assignments and use a concordancing program to analyse examples of learners' language looking for typical error patterns. Systematic errors in learners' writing can be used as a basis for the development of learning materials. Alternatively, a teacher might look through established corpora of texts by native speakers of the target language and find examples for patterns and present these to learners as examples or adapt them into exercises. Learners themselves can be trained in the use of a concordancing program and corpora, then become their own researchers finding examples and developing their own rules for grammatical structures, idioms and general usage, for example, investigating the differences between "look" and "see." This approach is often called Data Driven Learning.

2 Computer-Mediated Communication

컴퓨터를 활용한 의사소통은 컴퓨터 매개 의사소통(CMC)이라고 불리며, CALL과 연관된 활동 중 가장 잘 알려져 있다. CMC는 이메일, 게시판, 채팅과 MOO를 모두 포함하는데, 이것 자체가 언어 학습을 반드시 동반하는 것은 아니지만 목표어로 의미 협상을 할 때 언어 학습이 일어나게 된다. 이때 영어 교사들은 서로 다른 나라의 학생들이 CMC를 통해 목표어로 의사소통하는 과제를 제공할 수 있다.

Communicating using the computer is often referred to as computer-mediated communication(CMC) and is one of the more popular activities associated with CALL. CMC encompasses communication by email, bulletin boards, chat lines and within MOO(Multi-user domains, Object-oriented) environments. CMC refers to a situation in which computer-based discussion may take place but without necessarily involving learning. Of course, opportunities for learning are inherently present, especially in situations in which learners need to engage in negotiation of meaning with native speakers of the target language or even with peers of non-native proficiency. It is common for teachers in different countries to create assignments for their students to communicate in a common target language, for example, students in Korea and Brazil both learning English working together to collect information about each other's interests and studies.

(1) Asynchronous Mode

학습자들이 동시에 인터넷에 접속할 필요 없이 컴퓨터를 매개로 한다. 따라서 학습자 간의 의사소통에는 시간차(time gap)가 존재하는데, e-mail이나 bulletin board 등이 이에 해당한다.

Ex keypal project

e-mail을 활용한 keypal project는 특히 다른 문화권의 같은 또래나 비슷한 수준의 학생들과 메일을 주고받는다는 점에서 문화를 초월한 의사소통을 가능하게 한다.

Keypals is the term for pen pals who use email to communicate and provides a simple and effective way of putting learners in touch with other learners in other parts of the world. Learners can talk about their experiences of learning English, and email is the perfect medium for cross-cultural communication.

• Example of Keypal Project •

Keypal Project: Learners around the world	
Theme	Learning English, other countries and cultures
Aim	To find out about another country and what it's like learning English there
Learners	Young learners and adult learners, elementary level and higher
Suggested time frame	5 lessons of 1 hour each

Procedure	
Before starting the project	• Contact a teacher in another country and exchange detailed information about your classes. • Decide exactly how you will pair up your learners with the other teachers' learners, and whether pairs will be using their own email account.
Lesson 1	1. Pairwork using the Internet. Tell your learners that they will be contacting leaners in another country. First, they will need to find out some basic information about that country. 2. Brainstorm what learners already know about the country and give each group a topic to research. Give them a time limit to find out as much as they can.
Lesson 2	3. Write an introductory email. Tell your learners the name of the keypal they will be sending their email to. Learners compose an email to this keypal including information about themselves and their country, and the questions. 4. Check and revise the email. Learners now exchange their draft email with classmates for checking. As the email will be sent to another country and to someone they don't know, learners are usually very keen for their email to be as 'correct' as possible. 5. Learners correct their email and send the email to their keypal.
Lesson 3	6. Learners receive and read their emails. 7. Learners write a short reply thanking their keypal, and answering the questions in the email. Again, learners check and revise their emails before sending.
Lesson 4	8. Learners receive and read their second emails to prepare a poster or presentation describing what they have learnt about the other country.
Lesson 5	9. Learners in their small groups present their findings to the class. At the end of all the presentations, you could have the class vote 'prizes' for whose presentation was the most.
Suggested follow-up activities	Information on what learners have found out about the other country can be presented using other ICT tools such as a blog or a wiki. A cultural box of real objects can be posted to the partner class.

(2) Synchronous Mode

학습자들이 컴퓨터와 인터넷을 매개로 의사소통하기 위해서는 동시간대에 인터넷에 접속해야 한다. 즉각적인 상호작용과 피드백이 이뤄진다는 장점이 있지만 시간과 공간의 제약을 받는다는 단점도 있다.

Ex chat programs, video conferencing

(3) MOO

비동시성과 동시성 모드를 결합한 방식으로, 인터넷에 존재하는 가상공간이다. 즉, 게시판에 글을 올릴 수도 있고 서로 메일 혹은 쪽지를 주고받을 수 있는 비동시성의 특징을 지니면서, MOO에서 실시간 대화도 가능하다는 점에서 동시성의 특징도 지닌다.

MOO stands for 'multi-user object-oriented dimension.' It is a permanent space on the Internet set aside for a specific group, a virtual environment. You could call it an online community.

 In the Classroom

Getting Learners Involved in Conferencing on a MOO

The first step in getting learners involved in learning on a MOO is to get them involved in a conferencing, which allows both teacher and student to keep files of what has been said. The procedure is as follows:

1. Introduce the students to the basics of MOOing. Take the class to a MOO in small groups and have them communicate with each other so they get used to the unique environment.
2. Collect the first drafts of an essay from the students (via email). Have a copy of the draft with you for reference during the conference (either printed out or on-screen in a separate window).
3. Set up conferences for each student. Ask the students to bring three questions regarding their essay to the conference.
4. Meet each student at the MOO to discuss the draft, focusing on questions they bring.
5. Through non-verbal gestures, encourage the student to do most of the 'talking.'
6. Lead the students to state clearly by the end of the conference what they will focus on during the revision process.
7. Have the students save a log of the conversation to their hard drive or a floppy disk, or do it yourself and send it to the student in an email message.

➡ The advantages of such environments to learning a language is that a learner can enter into an environment where a target language is being spoken and be forced to react to others' words and actions.

⑷ Computer-adaptive Testing(CAT)

CAT는 각 시험의 난이도를 학습자의 능력에 맞추는 평가이다. 학습자들은 컴퓨터를 통해 시험을 치르며, 컴퓨터가 각 문항을 즉각적으로 채점하면서 그 다음 문항은 학습자의 단계에 따라 다르게 주어진다. 주어진 문제를 맞히면 그 다음 문제도 더 어려운 것이 주어지고, 주어진 문제를 틀리면 다음 문제는 더 쉬운 것이 주어진다.

CAT의 큰 장점은 대규모 교실에서도 학습자들은 각자 자신의 능력에 따라 맞춤화된 다른 시험을 보게 된다는 것이다. 그러나 CAT를 개발하는 것이 쉽지 않다는 것과, 학습자들은 이미 한 번 응답한 것에 대해서는 다시 볼 수 없고 답을 바꿀 수도 없다는 한계가 있다.

Computer-adaptive testing(CAT) uses a database of questions to match the difficulty of each test item to the abilities of the learners being tested. Learners take a CAT test at the computer and because the computer can instantly mark each answer, the following question can be tailored or adapted. If a learner correctly answers a question, the computer will ensure that the next question will be more difficult. If a learner incorrectly answers a question, the next question will be easier.

One of the great advantages of CAT testing is that randomization of test items can ensure that learners of a large class taking a test in the same room may all take slightly different tests as their correct and incorrect answers prompt the computer to take them to different levels. However, the effort in setting up CAT testing is also difficult and learners may not like the fact that they cannot review or change the answers to any questions they have already answered.

Plus ⊕

디지털 리터러시 활용 수업(Digital Literacy Learning)

디지털 리터러시란 컴퓨터, 인터넷과 같은 사이버상에서 찾아낸 정보의 가치를 평가할 수 있는 비판적인 사고력을 의미하며, 다양한 출처에서 찾은 여러 가지 형태의 정보를 이해하고 자신의 목적에 맞는 새로운 정보를 조합해 올바르게 사용하는 능력을 말한다(Gilster, 1997).

디지털 리터러시는 컴퓨터 리터러시(computer literacy), 정보 리터러시(information literacy), 지식 리터러시(knowledge literacy)를 포함하며 이는 각각 ICT 접근 능력, 활용 능력, 정보 생산 능력을 말한다. 인터넷과 다양한 디지털 기술을 활용할 경우, 목표 언어 국가의 가상 문화 체험, 원어민 발음, 상호작용적인 대화 등 멀티미디어 학습 자료를 활용한 자연스러운 상호작용을 통해 의사소통 능력을 향상시킬 수 있으며, 세계적인 감각까지도 배양할 수 있는 장점이 있다(한종임, 2008).

또한 디지털 리터러시 활용 수업은 서책형 자료와 다르게 다양한 멀티미디어 자료를 학생들이 이용할 수 있고 교사, 학생, 컴퓨터 간 다방향 학습을 통해 자기주도 학습이 가능하다는 장점도 있다. 이 밖에도 다양한 멀티미디어를 활용해 영어를 가르칠 경우 시간과 공간의 제약을 받지 않고 의사소통의 기회를 제공할 수 있기 때문에 학생들에게 의사소통 향상의 기회를 많이 부여할 수 있으며, 학생들이 유의미한 과업과 활동에 적극적으로 참여할 수 있어 학습의 효율성을 높일 수 있고, 그림이나 동영상과 같은 시청각적인 요소를 함께 제공함으로써 학생들의 동기를 높이는 장점도 있다(Chang, 2003).

Paul Gilster defines digital literacy as "the ability to understand and use information in multiple formats from a wide variety of sources when it is presented via computers" and, particularly, through the medium of the Internet (Gilster, in Pool 1997:6).

> ▶ **CD-ROM**
> CD-ROM은 비디오, 텍스트, 사진 및 사운드를 사용해 4 skills를 통합한 활동을 제공한다. 네 가지 언어 기술 모두에 연습을 통합하는 특수 기능을 갖추고 있다는 점에서 교사와 학습자 모두에게 잠재적으로 해당되는 도구이다. 컴퓨터 기반 학습은 학습자에게 동기를 부여하고 학습을 촉진하는 다양한 증거들이 있다. 특히 컴퓨터를 이용한 상호작용(interactive learning)은 컴퓨터를 학습 도구로 사용하는 교육학적 이점이다.
>
> CD-ROM is potentially a liberating instrument for teachers and learners alike in that it has the special facility of incorporating practice in all four language skills in a multimedia package using video, text, photograph and sound. There is much evidence, not least teachers' own experience, to suggest that computer-based learning is very motivating for children. However, teachers and researchers have to measure the pedagogical value of using a computer as opposed to any other tool in the promotion of learning (Hammond, 1994). Reeves (1995) in an article on "A model of the effective dimensions of interactive learning," emphasizes the need to prove the pedagogical advantages of using computers as a tool for learning.

Differentiated Instruction

Differentiated Instruction

개별화 수업이란 학생 개개인의 배움 수준, 언어 수준, 읽고 쓰는 능력 차이에 중점을 두고 커리큘럼과 수업 활동을 적용하는 것을 의미한다. 교사는 학생 수준에 맞춰 차등적인 학습 지원을 제공하지만 학생들 간의 극명한 수준 차이로 학습 동기를 저해하지 않도록 주의가 필요하다. 쉽고 어려운 활동을 차별적으로 제공하기보다는 하나의 활동 중 필요한 지식의 종류에 차등을 두거나 개별 학습과 협동 학습을 적절히 활용하도록 한다. 또 유연한 교실 상황을 조성해 학생들이 스스로 느끼는 수준 차이를 최소화하도록 도와야 한다.

Differentiated instruction is really about taking account of significant differences among students in terms of their ability (or disability), rate of learning, language proficiency, literacy and numeracy skills—and then using this knowledge to adapt the way the curriculum and learning activities are presented. These differences also determine the amount of additional support individual students may need.

It is very important that the teacher differentiate instruction correctly. The teacher should try not to level activities at all but to differentiate them using multiple intelligences instead. He/she also needs to give students the choice of what they want to do and how they want to work (self, partner, group) through the use of flexible grouping. That way everyone is different so no one feels different.

01 \ Mixed Level Class

1 Class Size – Large Classes

대부분의 교사들은 언어 학습의 가장 큰 걸림돌 중 하나를 대집단(large classes) 수업이라고 지적한다. 그러나 현장에 있는 교사들은 이와 같은 대집단 수업, 즉, 학생 수에 변화를 주기 어려운 학습 상황에 직면하고 있으므로 주어진 대집단 수업이라는 학습 상황에서의 효율성과 변화를 고려해 볼 수밖에 없다.

(1) Use Pairwork and Groupwork

학생들의 참여를 극대화하도록 대집단 수업을 짝 활동과 소집단 활동으로 구성하도록 한다.

When using pairwork and groupwork with large groups, it is important to make instructions especially clear, to agree how to stop the activity and to give good feedback.

(2) Maximize Individual Work

학생 개인의 속도와 능력에 맞춰 과제를 제공하도록 한다.

Perhaps we can get students to use graded readers as part of their individual reading programme. When we get students to build their own portfolio of work, we are asking them to work as individuals, too. We can encourage students to make full use of a school library or self-access centre. We can get students to write individually—offering their own responses to what they read and hear. We can direct them to language learning websites, or we can get them to produce their own blogs.

(3) Use Students

수업 중에 학생들마다 다른 책임감을 심어 주도록 한다.

For example, we can appoint class monitors whose job is to collect homework or hand out worksheets. Students can take the register or organize their classmates into groups. We can ask some of our students to teach the others.

This might mean asking individuals to be in charge of a group who are preparing arguments for a debate for example, or who are going through a worksheet. It might mean telling individual students that it is their job to explain some language to their group. We need to choose our student 'leaders' with care, and we will then monitor their performance very carefully. This will not only be useful for us, but may give them some satisfaction, too, and this may affect their motivation very positively.

(4) Use a Different Pace for Different Activities

소집단 수업에 비해 대집단 수업에서는 어렵지만, 가급적 과업마다 속도를 조절하도록 한다.

If we ask students to say something in a large class, for example, we need to give them time to respond before charging ahead. If we care conducing drills, we may be able to work at quite a fast pace, but if we are asking student to think about something, we will want to slow the pace right down.

2) Managing Mixed Level Class

대집단 수업의 가장 큰 문제점 중 하나는 학생들의 언어능력에 차이가 있다는 것이다. 따라서 혼합된 능력을 지닌 학생들(mixed ability students)을 지도하는 것은 교사에게 수업에 대한 계획 및 수행상의 여러 가지 문제점을 일으킨다.

Many teachers see mixed level classes as especially problematic. Yet in a real sense all classes have students with a mixture of different abilities and language levels. Within the school environments, students are often streamed—that is re-grouped for language lessons according to their abilities. In other situations, however, such placement and streaming are not possible and so teachers are faced with individuals who have different language knowledge, different intelligences, different learning speeds, and different learning styles and preferences. There is particular concern for the needs not only for students who are having difficulty at the lower end of the scale, but also for "gifted" students.

(1) Communicative Teaching Principles

의사소통적 언어 교수 원리를 토대로 mixed level class를 지도하기 위한 두 가지 전제는 다음과 같다.

① If students complete the task we set—answering a certain number of questions, marking a given number of sentences true or false—we feel that they have read or listened successfully.

② With a long, complex text, a simple task makes the reading or listening achievable for weaker students. With a shorter, simpler text, the task can be more demanding.

> Text level of challenge + Task level of support = Student success

(2) Different Student Actions

학생들에게 상이한 자료 및 내용을 제공하기 어려울 경우, 동일한 자료에 대한 상이한 반응 및 답변을 유도하는 것도 하나의 방법이다.

① **Give students different tasks**: 동일한 읽기 자료를 제공하고 학생들에게 저마다 다른 답변을 요구한다.

For example, group A might have to interpret the information in the text by reproducing it in graphic form (or in charts and tables). Group B, on the other hand, might answer a series of open-ended questions. Group C—the group we perceive as having the greatest need of support—might be offered a series of multiple-choice questions; their task is to pick the correct response from two or more alternatives because we think this will be easier for them than having to interpret all the information themselves.

② **Give students different roles**: 과제 진행 시 학생들에게 저마다 다른 역할을 제시한다.

If students are doing a role-play, for example, in which a police officer is questioning a witness, we might give the student playing the police officer the questions they should ask, whereas the student playing the witness has to come up with their own way of expressing what they want to say. We will have done this because the student or students playing the police officer clearly need more guidance than the others. If students are preparing for a debate, we might give Group A a list of suggested arguments to prepare from whereas Group B(whom we think need less support) are told to come up with their own arguments.

③ **Reward early finishers**: 동일한 내용의 과제를 일찍 마친 그룹에게는 관련된 추가 과제를 제공해 흥미와 동기 유발을 유지하도록 한다.

④ **Encourage different student responses**: 동일한 자료와 과제를 제공하되, 학생들의 능력에 따른 결과물(outcome)을 유도할 수 있다.

We can pick up flexible tasks which make virtue out of differences between students. For example, we ask students to write some true statements containing the words *in, tomorrow, my, hope, the moon* and *five*. Each sentence must contain one of these words, and the maximum number of sentences is 12. The more proficient students have a clear but high target to aim for, but everyone, including those who are not so able, have something purposeful to do.

(3) What the Teacher Does

Mixed level class를 운영하는 교사들은 학생들의 학습 결손을 막기 위한 방법으로 학생들의 능력을 배치고사(placement test)나 진단고사(diagnostic test) 등을 통해 수준별(ability grouping) 소집단으로 나눠 언어 학습을 진행하거나, whole class로 진행하되 학생들의 수준에 따라 과제의 결과를 다르게 유도하는 교수 전략을 사용하기도 한다.

① **Responding to students**: 수업 중 교사는 학생 활동에 따라 빈번하게 반응하며 적절한 피드백을 제공하는데, 이때 가급적 학생 개개인의 수준을 고려해 보다 세심한 설명 및 피드백을 제공해야 한다.

Students who are experiencing difficulty may need us to help them clear up some problems; we might have to correct some language use, or help them to organize information logically, for example. If they are working on a webquest on the Internet, we might have to show them which link to follow or what to do next. This kind of flexible response is one of the main aspects of differentiation.

② **Being inclusive**: Mixed level class의 가장 큰 문제점 중 하나는 일부 학생들이 수업에 뒤처져 있거나 참여하지 않는다는 것이다.

If we spend a lot of time with the higher-levels students in a class, the students who are less linguistically able may feel that they are being ignored and become demotivated as a result. If, on the other hand, we spend all our time with students who we think need our help more than others, the higher-level students may feel neglected and unchallenged. Such students quickly lose interest in the class and develop an attitude which makes them difficult to work with.

③ Mixed level class의 교사들은 모든 학생들이 수업에 참여할 수 있도록 유도해야 한다.

When setting a task with the whole group (perhaps by asking initial questions to build up a situation), teachers will want to start by working at a level that all of the students are comfortable with. She will ask questions that all the students can understand and relate to so that their interest is aroused and so that they all the students can understand the goal they are aiming for. Once they are all involved with the topic or the task, she may allow for differentiation in any of the ways. But her initial task is to include and engage everyone—because students who feel they are excluded will soon start to behave as if they are excluded!

④ **Flexible groupings**: 과제의 성격과 유형에 따라 다양하게 학생들을 소집단 활동으로 유도할 수 있다.

Sometimes we might put them different groups so that each group can do different tasks. We might group them so that different groups can read different texts, depending on the difficulty of the texts. At other times, however, we might put students at different levels in the same group because we believe that the weaker students will benefit from working with students at a higher linguistic level and because, at the same time, we believe the higher-level students will gain insights about the language, for example, by having to explain it to their peers.

(4) Language Experience Approach

Example ①

교사가 집단으로부터 이야기를 이끌어 내면서 보다 능력 있는 학습자들은 수정하거나 단어의 철자를 말하는 교사의 역할을 맡는다.

Bell also suggests starting the story with contributions from the emergent reader/writers, and ending it with contributions from the more advanced students. This way, follow-up activities can be done that are appropriate to each level using different portions of the story.

Example ②

학생들이 짝 활동을 통해 texts를 만들어 낸다. 교사는 다음의 절차를 이용할 수 있다.

- Set up an event that could be used for language experience.

or

- Have students think of an important event in their lives in the last (week, month, year).
- Practice telling the story silently to themselves; ask students to think through the beginning, middle, and ending, as well as key points in the story.
- Pair more literate learners with those with limited literacy skills. Have them tell their story to their partner.

- More literate leaners write the story as it is told to them. Those with limited literacy skills can draw pictures or verbally recount what they have understood. These verbal accounts could be tape-recorded and used for other class activities.
- Student-generated texts are then used by the whole class for other practice activities.

(5) Pairing and Grouping Students

짝과 집단을 정할 때 능력 차이가 가장 명백한 요소가 될 수 있지만 성별, 가족 관계, 학습자 기대, 활동 목적 등에 따라 여러 가지 요소를 고려할 수 있다.

There are benefits to both like-ability and cross-ability pairs and groups.

① Advantages to like-ability groupings

   ⓐ Beginning-level learners can participate more openly with students at a similar level.

   ⓑ The advanced level students need to be more challenged if working with others at an advanced level as well.

② Advantages to cross-ability groupings

   ⓐ Stronger students provide beginning-level students with valuable language input.

   ⓑ Helping others and acting as a peer tutor has value as well, but it is important that the learners perceive that there is a benefit to taking on this leadership role.

Example

1. Have more advanced learners ask the questions in an interview activity.
2. Have more literate students transcribe stories of emergent reader/writer.
3. Have more advanced students give verbal instructions to beginning-level students, who arrange pictures, complete an information gap, etc. The input is likely to be comprehensible to the beginner.
4. In jigsaw activities, give the higher-level learners more demanding questions to answer.

02 \ Task Types for Mixed Level Teaching

1 Tiered Tasks

수준별 그룹으로 진행하되, 과업 수행 결과물은 유사하다.

Example 1

다음은 'The spirit of London'이라는 읽기 자료를 토대로 구성된 3개의 과업 자료이다.

Top Tier

Task A: for weaker students

1. How much of London's history does *The spirit of London* show?
2. How do you go around it?
3. What special effects does it have?
4. What can you see in the modern-day section?

Answers

ⓐ light, sound, music, and smells   ⓑ police, punks, and tourist

ⓒ more than 400 years   ⓓ in a taxi

Middle Tier

Task B: for midlevel students

1. How much of London's history does *The spirit of London* show?
   ⓐ 400 years   ⓑ more than 400 years   ⓒ 300 years

2. How do you go around it?
   ⓐ in a taxi   ⓑ in a train   ⓒ on foot

3. What special effects does it have?
   ⓐ lights   ⓑ sound and music   ⓒ smells

4. What can you see in the modern-day section?
   ⓐ police   ⓑ punks   ⓒ tourists

> **Bottom Tier**
>
> Task C: for stronger students
>
> 1. How much of London's history does *The spirit of London* show?
> 2. How do you go around it?
> 3. What special effects does it have?
> 4. What can you see in the modern-day section?

- Matching work: Task A gives all the answers on the page for support. They are jumbled for challenge. Weaker students manipulate the given material, and can use logic to help match the task items, together with the information in the reading text.
- Multiple choice questions: Task B gives multiple-choice answers to help the average students. This is slightly different from the conventional "one answer only is correct" multiple choice, since in questions 3 and 4 there are more than one correct answer.
- Open questions: Task C gives open questions—with no extra support—to challenge the stronger students in the group.

Example ❷

07

Tiered task의 보다 간단한 형태로 학생들의 수준을 두 단계로 나눠 동일한 과업을 진행하되, 교사가 과업의 support를 다르게 제공한다. Dual-choice gapfill이 이에 해당한다.

The Dead Sad Animal Rap	MISSING WORDS
Listen to the rap. What are the missing words?	killed / shot
Humans... ⓐ ... the dear old dodo,	easy / simple
It was... ⓑ ... It couldn' fly	hunted / shot
Humans... ⓒ ... all the passenger pigeons	south / north
From the... ⓓ ... American sky.	

As they listen, weaker students circle one of the words in the box to fill each gap. Stronger students get the same task sheet, but with the missing words box cut off. The task is therefore more challenging for them.

2 Bias Tasks

그룹을 mixed level로 구성하되, 학생들의 수준에 따라 역할 비중을 다르게 하거나 서로 다른 과업을 주도록 한다.

Example 1

다음은 학생들이 Penpal Ad Page를 읽고 진행할 과업들이다.

Task A: for weaker students
1. How many of the young people are 13 years old? (Three...)
2. How many boys are there?
3. Who doesn't eat meat?
4. Who likes football?
5. Who lives in the country?

Task B: for stronger students
Write questions for these answers, based on the Penpal Page.
1. How many of them are 13? Three of them are.
2. _____? There are four.
3. _____? Eloise doesn't.
4. _____? James does.
5. _____? Chris does.

With task A, weaker students answer questions about the text. With Task B, stronger students write questions for given answers related to the text. Because the answers to these two tasks are complementary, it would not be an efficient use of class time for the teacher to conduct post-activity feedback with the whole class. Instead, student-students feedback would be a good idea, with the students in AB pairs. The teacher should naturally be available as an arbiter if there are any questions of their own. If they are grammatically correct, and fit the given answers, the teacher should confirm them as also correct. This type of feedback, in weak/strong pairs, is very motivating for the weaker students. They have got the difficult questions that the strong students have struggled to reconstruct. For weak students, already knowing key information is a pleasant change from traditional whole-class oral feedback, which often turns into a dialogue between the teacher and the brightest and most forthcoming students.

Example ❷

보다 간단한 bias task의 유형은 jigsawed gapfill의 형태이다. 주로 노래(song)나 이야기(short episode)를 들려주고 학생들에게 요약된 복사본을 주되, 학생들의 수준에 따라 higher-level students(Task sheet A)에게는 보다 많은 빈칸으로 구성된 복사본을 주고 weaker students(Task sheet B)에게는 빈칸이 상대적으로 적은 복사본을 제공하도록 한다. 이때 각 복사본 A, B의 빈칸은 서로 다른 장소가 지워져 있어야 한다.

The simplicity or complexity of the words you gap can also make the task easier or more difficult. A positive feature of this kind of bias activity is that because the jigsawed gaps are in different places, students are not necessarily aware of who has more gaps and who has fewer.

▶ **Action Research** is any systematic inquiry conducted by teacher researchers to gather information about the ways that their particular school operates, how they teach, and how well their students learn. The information is gathered with the goals of gaining insight, developing reflective practice, effecting positive changes in the school environment and on educational practices in general, and improving student outcomes.

07

Reference

- 교육부(1997) 제7차 교육과정 중학교 영어과 교육과정 해설, 서울:대한교과서
- 교육부(1997) (제7차) 외국어과 (I), 서울:교육부
- 김영숙 외 5인(1999) 영어과 교육론, 서울:한국문화사
- 김덕기(1998) 영어 교육론, 서울:고려대학교출판부
- 이흥수(1999) 영어 평가 및 멀티미디어 교육론, 서울:한국문화사
- 최연희 외 2인(1998) 열린 교육을 위한 중학교 영어/수학 수행평가의 적용과 효과에 대한 분석 연구, 서울:이화여자대학교사범대학
- Anderson, Anne & Lynch, Tony (2001) Listening:OUP
- Betsy Parrish (2011) Teaching Adult ESL(Practical Introduction):McGrawHill
- Brown, H. Douglas (2000) Principles of Language Learning and Teaching, Fourth Edition:Pearson Education
- Brown, H. Douglas (2001) Teaching by Principles, An Interactive Approach to Language Pedagogy, Second Edition:Pearson Education
- Brown, H. Douglas (2002) Strategies for Success, A Practical Guide to Learning English:Longman
- Brown, H. Douglas (2004) Language Assessment, Principle and Classroom Practices:Longman
- Brumfit, C. J. and Johnson, K (1994) The Communicative Approach to Language Teaching:OUP
- Byrne, Donn (1994) Teaching Oral English, Essex:Longman
- Cross, David (2001) A Practical Handbook Of Language Teaching, Fourth Impression:Longman
- Celce—Murcia, Marianne (2001) Teaching English as a Second or Foreign Language, Third Edition:Heinle & Heinle
- Cook, Guy (2000) Discourse:OUP
- Davies, Paul and Pearse, Eric (2002) Success in English Teaching, Second Impression:OUP
- Ellis, Rod (1999) Understanding Second Language Acquisition:OUP
- Hadley, Alice Omaggio (2001) Teaching Language in Context, Third Edition:Heinle & Heinle
- Heaton, J. B. (1990) Classroom Testing:Longman

- Hedge, Tricia (2000) Teaching and Learning in the Language Classroom:OUP
- Lankshear, Colin, and Michelle Knobel (2006) Digital Literacy and Digital Literacies: Policy, Pedagogy and Research Considerations for Education:Digital Kompetanse
- Larsen-Freeman, Diane (2000) Techniques and Principles in Language Teaching, Second Edition:OUP
- Littlewood, William (1981) Communicative Language Teaching: CUP
- Lightbown and Spada (2003) How Language are Learned, Third Edition:OUP
- Lynch, Tony (1997) Communication in the Language:OUP
- McCarthy, Michael (2001) Discourse Analysis for Language Teachers:CUP
- Nunan, David (2000) Language Teaching Methodology:Pearson Education
- Nunan, David (2003) Practical English Language Teaching:McGraw Hill
- Richard-Amato, Patrica A. (2003) Making It Happen, From Interactive to Participatory Language Teaching, Theory and Practice:Third Edition:Longman
- Richard, Jack C. and Nunan David (1997) Second Language Teacher Education:CUP
- Richard, Jack C. (1995) Understanding Communication In Second Language Classroom:CUP
- Richard, Jack C. and Rogers, Theodore S. (2002) Approaches and Methods in Language Teaching:CUP
- Richard, Jack C. and Schmidt (2002) Dictionary of Language Teaching & Applied Linguistics, Third Edition:Longman
- Shrum, Judith L. and Gilsan, Eileen W. (2000) Teacher's Handbook: Contextualized Language Instruction, Second Edition:Heinle & Heinle
- Teeler, Dede with Gray, Peta (2001) How to Use the Internet in ELT, Third Edition:Longman
- Thornbury, Scott (2000) How to Teach Grammar:Longman
- Thornbury, Scott (2000) How to Teach Vocabulary:Longman
- Ur, Penny (1998) Teaching Listening Comprehension:CUP
- Ur, Penny (2002) A Course in Language Teaching:CUP

NEW

Build Up

박현수 영어교육론 ①-1

Guideline for Pre-service Teachers

Theoretical Background for Classroom Teaching

초판인쇄 | 2025. 1. 10. **초판발행** | 2025. 1. 15. **편저자** | 박현수

발행인 | 박 용 **발행처** | (주)박문각출판 **표지디자인** | 박문각 디자인팀

등록 | 2015년 4월 29일 제2019-000137호

주소 | 06654 서울시 서초구 효령로 283 서경빌딩 **팩스** | (02)584-2927

전화 | 교재주문·학습문의 (02)6466-7202

정가 31,000원(1, 2권 포함)
ISBN 979-11-7262-417-0 | ISBN 979-11-7262-416-3(세트)